Katherine

its a bit old, but may be useful,

Jenny

THE
TEENAGE VEGETARIAN SURVIVAL GUIDE

D1189121

THE
TEENAGE VEGETARIAN SURVIVAL GUIDE

Anouchka Grose with Ruth Jones

Illustrated by Susannah English

Foreword by Juliet Gellatley
Campaigns Director of The Vegetarian Society

RED FOX

A Red Fox Book

Published by Random Century Children's Books
20 Vauxhall Bridge Road, London SW1V 2SA

A division of the Random Century Group
London Melbourne Sydney Auckland
Johannesburg and agencies throughout the world

First published by Red Fox 1992

Typeset in 10½/12pt Century Old Style by
Falcon Typographic Art Ltd, Edinburgh
Printed in Great Britain by
Cox & Wyman Ltd, Reading

ISBN 0 09 987360 5

CONTENTS

*The editors and consultants would like
to dedicate this book to the memory of
Ros
A dedicated worker for animal rights and
co-founder of
CALF*

Thanks to
Pam Tinsley and Fergus Duff
at the Vegetarian Society
for answering all my stupid questions.

Juliet Gellatley at The Vegetarian Society
for checking the manuscript and
for all her helpful comments and advice.

Dad
For being such a constructive critic.

Philip and Laura
For the loan of the library cards.

Louise
For the bike lock.

Karen
For reading bits.

No thanks to
V
For trying so hard to stop me working.

FOREWORD

I know it's a few years ago but I can remember very clearly what it was like to be 15. It was then I decided to become a vegetarian.

When I told my mum her reaction couldn't have been any different if I'd said I was going to sail round the world with the Manchester United football team, invite 27 homeless bongo players to live in our house and have all my teeth out so I never had to go to the dentist again. She was not very pleased.

According to her I was going to drop dead from malnutrition and what's more, under no circumstances was she going to cook two meals every night.

Funny how times change. Now my sister and brother are also veggies and my mum says she 90 per cent of the way there! My dad? Don't even ask about him. He's still a meat eater but at least he's a guilty one!

I became a vegetarian because I wanted stop the sickening cruelty and abuse which farm animals are put through. What brought it about was an open-day visit to a Government-owned farm – a so-called show piece farm. It was a place where farmers came to learn how to look after their own animals.

The creatures I remember most vividly are the pigs and hens. Before this, the only chickens I had ever seen were scratching around on a farmyard in the countryside. Here they weren't scratching around and it wasn't the countryside.

As I entered the shed where they were kept I had to strain my eyes to see in the gloomy interior. The stench of their droppings took my breath away and within minutes I had a blinding headache. Thousands of chickens were locked into tiny cages. They could barely move, they couldn't stretch their wings and some of them were dead. The noise was both deafening and disturbing. It was a picture of insanity.

The pigs were even more upsetting. Breeding sows were tethered by their necks in small metal stalls. They could not turn around, couldn't even take a step backwards or forwards and could only lie down with difficulty. And there were hundreds of them, all in solitary confinement.

In other stalls were three huge boars. One of them just looked at me – it looked and it looked, directly into my eyes. This intelligent, expressive creature seemed to be asking why. I couldn't give the answer because I didn't understand it myself. The only thing I could do was to cry and to keep saying that I was sorry, over and over again.

When I left that place I realized there *was* something I could do about it – I could make sure I didn't eat those pigs or those hens or any animals. I also decided there and then to work to end this exploitation.

That was a few years ago but my feelings haven't changed one bit. What has changed, though, is the number of people who think similarly. We now know that vegetarianism isn't just some kind of fad or hippy thing to do. It is the most important step you can take to improve your health, to save animals and to protect the planet.

Over the last year, vegetarianism has doubled to almost four million people. On top of that, 17 million people – that's one in three of the population – have cut out red meat (pigs, sheep and cows) altogether or have cut down on it dramatically.

The biggest growth area of people who refuse to eat animals is young people. You are the ones who have the wisdom and sense to understand what is happening to our world and the compassion to do something about it. The decision you have taken is the most

positive and effective one possible. It will have an immediate effect in the fight against cruelty, exploitation, waste and greed.

Although you are not alone, it sometimes feels that way. In a world where meat eating is still the norm, all of us need support and help. If there are ever times when, under pressure from parents or stupid friends, your will power begins to weaken, this survival guide will sort you out!

If you ever wonder or worry about getting the right vitamins; you can't answer the ignorant questions people throw at you; or you're afraid your love life will go down the pan – read on!

Just as importantly, if you want to get active – get going! There's loads of other ways of working to help end animal cruelty and they're in this book.

You've taken the first and most difficult step so don't let anyone talk you out of it. Be proud to be veggie, stand up for what you believe and never apologize for doing what's right.

Juliet Gellatley
Campaigns Director
The Vegetarian Society

Part One

THEORY

1

WHAT IS A
VEGETARIAN?

It's all very well making a song and dance about giving up meat and being kind to animals, but what exactly is a vegetarian? There are plenty of misguided people out there who think that veggies either have to be eccentric health-food freaks or pathalogical animal lovers.

They couldn't be more wrong! Vegetarians come in all sorts of shapes, sizes and colours – fat, thin, young, old, black, white, yellow. The combinations are endless. Just remember, the great thing is that at the end of the day, anyone can be a vegetarian – including YOU!

Every week in the UK twenty-eight thousand people become vegetarian. So you're in great company.

Taking the plunge

Most people seem to take a while to go fully vegetarian, once they've taken the initial decision. Rather than giving up everything straight away, you may decide to cut things out a bit at a time. That's a perfectly reasonable approach. There's no rush, so take things slowly. You may decide to drop all red meat from your diet initially, then perhaps cut out white meat and, finally, stop eating fish. Feel free to take your time and adjust your eating habits as and when you can.

Types of conscientious eaters

Let's have a look at the different types of people who make choices about their food and see which category you fit into.

Fish-eaters

Quite a few people who give up meat (including poultry) carry on eating fish. In a way this is a perfectly valid and understandable thing to do. If you are giving up mainly for health reasons then fish is, technically at least, less bad for you than meat (see Chapter Three). But if you're giving up for moral/animal rights' reasons you must remember that fish have feelings too and are just as capable of suffering as other creatures. Fish are sometimes farmed and kept in overcrowded cages. Even when they are caught in the wild, they are often left to gasp to death slowly in the open air. And even if you have no sympathy for fish at all, think of all the whales that are killed by fishermen

because they eat too many fish and so interfere with the fishing industry – not to mention the sharks and dolphins that are caught by mistake in those huge industrial fishing nets.

Not only do fish suffer because people like eating them, but also they may not be as healthy as you might think, which is another good reason for giving them up. Get hold of a copy of The Vegetarian Society's leaflet *Why There Aren't Plenty More Fish in The Sea.* It explains why it's unhealthy to eat fish caught from polluted oceans, how fish suffer agonizing deaths and why eating fish is destroying the seas. (For The Vegetarian Society's address see p. 152.)

Non-meat eaters

There are many people who don't eat any meat or fish, but don't worry about eating animal fats and other non-vegetarian ingredients. Even if they have stopped eating fish or meat because they don't want to kill animals, they have no qualms about wearing a leather jacket, for instance.

Another unfussy sort of non-meat eater is the type that only eats meat outside the home. They might be quite a strict vegetarian when they cook for themselves, but when they eat out they'll eat whatever they're given.

100% lacto-ovo veggie

These are the only people who should really call themselves vegetarian. They opt for a diet that excludes meat, fish and poultry, and any slaughterhouse by-products like animal fat and gelatine.

As far as The Vegetarian Society is concerned, the definition of a true vegetarian is someone who eats no meat or meat products, poultry, fish or slaughterhouse by-products and who also only eats free-range eggs. When you learn how battery hens are treated and about the high proportion of deaths involved in producing battery eggs, you can see why they think this is important.

However, these veggies do include milk, cheese and eggs in their diet and so they are known as lacto-ovo vegetarians (from the latin words *lacto* and *ovo*, which mean milk and eggs).

Even though these type of veggies eat milk and eggs, they avoid eating battery-farmed eggs because of the cruelty involved. They also don't eat cheese which contains rennet. Rennet is made from the stomach lining of a slaughtered calf and is used to set cheese. Vegetarian cheese which does not contain rennet is available from health-food shops and most supermarkets.

Quite a few of those who are very veggie in the food department still wear leather shoes. This doesn't make complete sense (see p. 129 for arguments for and against) but a lot of people still do it, nonetheless.

Non-egg eating veggie

This is pretty self-explanatory, really. Quite a few vegetarians don't eat eggs, mainly because of battery farming but also partly because the male chicks have to be killed in order to build up a flock solely of egg-laying hens and because eggs contain large amounts of saturated fat and cholesterol, chemicals which are related to heart disease.

Vegan

A vegan is someone who follows a diet that excludes anything derived from animals, whether it kills the animal or not. As well as fish, meat and poultry they do not eat eggs, milk, cheese, butter, cream or honey. Vegans get all the protein they need from nuts, seeds, beans (and soya products) and cereals. This can be a very healthy way of eating, provided you do it properly and make sure you're not missing out on any vitamins and minerals.

If you do decide to go vegan it would be a good idea to get a vegan cookbook with a good nutrition section to make sure you have a varied diet. It's also probably not a good idea to go vegan straight away. Try being lacto-ovo vegetarian for a couple of months and cut out dairy foods gradually.

Remember: whatever sort of conscientious eater you choose to become is up to you. You'll be doing a good deal to make animals' lives happier and more humane if you just give up meat and battery eggs. It's totally up to you how far you want to go. The vast majority of vegetarians don't always manage to carry their commitment right down the line. Holidays, workplace food, other people's cooking often intervenes and means a bit of non-rennet cheese or a non-free-range egg has to be eaten every now and then. For the teenage veggie it can be even harder, because you're probably living in your parents' home and relying on their goodwill. Don't tie yourself into knots of anguish because you haven't been able to achieve all the commitment you'd like – and don't let anyone else tell you you're being illogical or hypocritical if you do use that bag you were given with a bit of leather in the handle or eat that creamy mousse with gelatine in – you're probably doing a sight more than they are to make the world a better place for animals, and that's what counts.

2

HUMANE REASONS FOR BEING VEGETARIAN

Moral and ethical reasons

Probably the most common reason why people decide to stop eating meat is because of their horror at the pain and suffering we inflict on animals in order to eat what we like, and the cruel ways in which we kill them.

It's not a pretty story . . .

Factory farming

Most of the 700 million animals slaughtered annually in the UK have spent their short, unhappy lives trapped in hideous, artificial conditions, unable to move freely, unable to see daylight or experience fresh air.

Factory farms are designed to achieve maximum production and the fastest growth of animals in as short a time as possible. It's far too costly to worry about animals' welfare: profit is the name of the game.

Here's how farm animals really spend their lives, before being carted off to the slaughterhouse . . .

Broiler chickens

Chickens reared for their meat are known as broiler chickens. 600 million broiler chickens are slaughtered each year in the UK – most of them are just seven weeks old when they meet their fate. Some chicks don't even survive their first day. About fifty million day-old chicks are killed every year in the UK as they are deemed unsuitable for the table – their bodies considered too lean.

Rearing broiler chickens entails thousands and thousands of chickens being put into windowless sheds. To have forty thousand chickens in one shed is not uncommon, and many can house up to one hundred thousand. The chickens are fed an intensive amount of growth promoters. The birds are also fed on dead chickens, turning them into cannibals. These animals could have been infected by scrapie or BSE (Bovine Spongiform Encephalopathy), two viral diseases which attack the brain.

As the chickens put on weight and grow, conditions become more and more cramped until the birds are unable to move. Many die from heart attacks or from being trampled on, while others suffer agonizing ammonia burns from being forced to stand in their own droppings. The ammonia that rises up from masses of droppings often blinds them, too.

It's easy to see how diseases are spread in these appalling conditions. Each year in the UK between twenty and thirty million birds die in the broiler shed, while two-and-a-half million die from suffocation and shock on their way to the slaughterhouse.

Pigs

Sows (female pigs) are kept in pens so small and uncomfortable that they are unable to turn round and sometimes even to lie down. They're also sometimes tethered around the neck or girth.

Wild pigs choose their mating partners, but on commercial farms there is no such thing as choice. All sows are locked into a device called a rape rack and serviced by the same boar. Then, throughout the whole of their sixteen-and-a-half-week pregnancy, they will be trapped in a stuffy shed with few or no windows.

Before a sow gives birth, she will be moved to a farrowing crate where she will try to make a nest in preparation for the arrival of her young. This is virtually impossible, as the animals have little or no bedding in their pens.

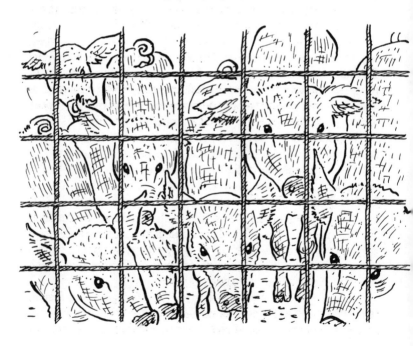

Once the piglets are born, they will be taken from their mother after just two or three weeks, and she will return to her stall about a week later, where the pregnancy process is repeated.

Once a sow is past her usefulness – usually after about five pregnancies – she will be killed for meat. In the meantime, the piglets will be fattened in dirty, overcrowded pens and finally killed when they are about six months old.

Veal

Like human mothers, cows produce milk to feed their young. But, unlike human mothers, cows usually have their offspring taken away from them just twenty-four hours after they've been born. The newly-born calf is put into a tiny wooden crate. Before long, it will be unable to stand properly or turn around in its cramped 'home', and will develop deformed joints.

Because people like their veal to be very white, the calves are fed solely on an iron-deficient liquid diet. This is to make them anaemic so that their meat is less 'bloody'. Then, when they are fourteen weeks old, the calves are slaughtered. Veal production of this sort has been outlawed in Britain in favour of more humane methods, but British calves are still exported in cramped, cruel conditions to countries like Holland and France, where this cruel practice is still legal. Their meat is then imported back to Britain!

An unhappy ending

More than 600 million chickens, 33.5 million turkeys, 14.2 million pigs, 20 million sheep, 3.5 million cattle and 5 million rabbits are slaughtered annually in the UK alone. And anyone who's seen a film of what goes on in a slaughterhouse will know that these animals are not killed humanely.

Animals are as alive as we are. They feel pain and fear in a similar way to us. There is no question that they approach a slaughterhouse in a state of abject terror and that the methods of transporting them to their deaths and actually killing them cause them great mental and physical suffering. Anyone who imagines that animals are killed for their meat in a quick and painless way is living in a dream world.

To the slaughterhouse

There are no happy endings in the slaughterhouse, and certainly no such thing as humane killing. Many animals, if they manage to survive the horrendous conditions they are reared in, fail to last during their fateful journey to the slaughterhouse.

Chickens are moved from the broiler house to the slaughterhouse lorry by 'catching' teams who grab the birds' legs – often causing dislocation and broken bones. Once packed into small crates aboard the lorry, poultry can suffocate in the heat in the summer months, freeze to death in the winter or simply die from shock.

Cattle and sheep suffer terrible mishandling and crowded conditions during their transportation to the slaughterhouse.

Those animals exported abroad for slaughter are subject to similar mistreatment, as well as long, arduous journeys over hundreds of miles with little or no food or water.

Poultry

On arrival at the slaughterhouse, the birds are hung upside-down in shackles. A conveyor belt transports them, fully conscious, to an electrically charged water bath which is supposed to stun them as their heads are dragged through it. But this useless method means that many birds are still alive when they reach the automatic knife which cuts their throats. This, too, is a very hit-and-miss method – the knife may fail to kill up to fifteen per cent of the birds, inflicting cruel wounds on them instead.

Finally, to prepare the birds for plucking, their bodies are plunged into a scalding tank. Many are boiled alive.

Cattle

Metal bolts are fired through the brains of cattle with a captive-bolt pistol. The pistol shot is supposed to render the animal unconscious before it is killed. In fact, this device often means more suffering because the terrified animal frequently struggles and makes the bolt miss the mark, causing even greater pain.

The animals are then hung upside-down, their throats are cut, and they are left to bleed to death.

Pigs and sheep

Most sheep and pigs are stunned by an electric charge before having their throats cut. Only – guess what? – this, too, is an inefficient method which may only knock the animal out for twenty seconds or so, leaving it fully conscious when the time comes for it to have its throat cut.

The Vegetarian Society reckons that during their lifetime the average vegetarian, by not eating meat or fish, prevents the suffering of 1000 animals.

3

HEALTH REASONS FOR BEING VEGETARIAN

Many people turn to a vegetarian lifestyle because of the health risks associated with eating meat and animal products.

If you eat a well-balanced veggie diet you can almost guarantee you'll be healthier than your meat-eating counterparts. There are no vitamins, minerals or proteins found in meat that can't be found elsewhere. What you *will* go without are the health risks involved in meat-eating. The diseases that can be prevented or improved by switching to a healthy, high fibre, low-fat vegetarian diet are:

Breast cancer	Kidney stones
Colon cancer	Obesity
Constipation	Osteoporosis
Diet-related diabetes	Ovarian cancer
Diverticulosis	Pancreatic cancer
Endometrial cancer	Peptic ulcers
Gallstones	Prostate cancer
Haemorrhoids	Salmonellosis
Heart disease	Stomach cancer
Hiatal hernias	Strokes
Hypertension	Trichinosis

The heart of the matter

Research has proved that a diet high in saturated fats – that's the sort found in meat, dairy food and eggs – is a contributory cause of heart disease, the commonest cause of death in most developed countries. In fact, Britain has one of the highest incidences of death from heart disease in the whole *world* – remember the great British fry-up?

A vegetarian diet, however, tends to be low in saturated fat and high in fibre (which helps prevent fats passing into the bloodstream). In meat there is little or no fibre. Red meat, dairy foods and eggs contain high levels of saturated fat, which can cause heart disease.

Consider these facts:

★ Five hundred people die from heart disease every day in Britain alone;

★ The average American man stands a fifty per cent chance of dying from a heart attack, whereas the risk for an average American vegetarian man is only fifteen per cent (and for a vegan only four per cent);

★ By halving the amount of meat and animal produce you eat it is reckoned you can reduce the chance of suffering a heart attack by forty-five per cent;

★ If you cut out animal produce altogether the risk decreases by ninety per cent.

Vegetarians spend on average twenty-two per cent less time in hospital than meat-eaters!

A high consumption of fresh fruit and vegetables is necessary in the diet and helps to prevent chronic and fatal diseases like heart disease and cancer because they contain essential protective nutrients.

Those who are in the meat business are there to make a profit. So they're not going to throw away any meat they can pass on to the public. All the unsavoury bits of head and insides – and small bones – are ground up, sold as cheap mince and usually end up being used by big institutions – like school canteens. Meat that has been condemned as unfit is often cut up and sold – so you could end up eating some disease-ridden, tapeworm-filled tubercular piece of meat next time you stop off for a cheap burger.

And if that isn't bad enough, what about the diseases you can actually *catch* from eating meat . . .

Chemicals

Eating meat means taking a whole lot of unhealthy chemicals into your body. Factory-farmed animals are routinely fed on high doses of growth stimulators and antibiotics, not to mention grain which has been heavily sprayed with pesticides.

> 95% of food poisoning is related to meat and poultry consumption.

Diseases

It seems rather odd that cows, who are herbivorous, should be fed offal – which is animal organs such as the heart and liver – but the practice used to be widespread in the UK. By feeding on bits of sheep or cattle, cows can contract mad cow disease, or BSE (Bovine Spongiform Encephalopathy). Cattle who catch BSE gradually go mad as their brains decay into a spongy mass. BSE in cows is always fatal.

> Crops fed to cattle are more heavily sprayed with pesticides than crops grown for human consumption. Most meat contains up to fourteen times as many pesticides as vegetable foods.

It is not yet clear whether humans can catch BSE by eating infected meat, as it can take at least twenty years for the symptoms to develop. However, this disease has been known to spread to other animals, including pigs and cats, who have eaten feed containing the infected flesh.

Many scientists are seriously concerned that BSE is a time-bomb waiting to explode on the meat-eating world. BSE is now killing three hundred cattle a week in the UK. What is going to happen when it spreads, as it may, to the humans who have eaten infected cows?

The meat industry has created this terrifying disease – is it any wonder that more and more people are turning towards vegetarianism?

White meat

Many people believe they'll be safe if they eat only white meat. Forget it!

Chicken pieces, such as wings or thighs, are often sold as pieces because they come from birds which are so diseased that they can't be sold whole.

Researchers at Leeds University found that almost eighty per cent of oven-ready chickens were contaminated with the bacteria salmonella, which isn't necessarily killed during cooking. Salmonella, which gives humans food-poisoning, is often caused by feeding dead chickens to broilers (chickens bred for their meat).

One in twenty pigs carry traces of sulphadimine, a growth-inducing drug, which is strongly suspected of causing cancer in humans.

4

Economic Reasons for Being Vegetarian

An estimated sixty million people around the world will die of starvation this year. Another five-hundred million will not get enough to eat. Yet the world has ample resources to feed its population – what's the problem?

Meat farming is a grossly inefficient method of food production, and is a major contributor to the world food shortage. Since over one-third of the world's grain is used to feed cattle (rather than humans) vast amounts of land is used to grow crops to feed them. But animals only convert about one-tenth of what they eat into protein, so they are wasting up to ninety per cent of what they eat as dung. This means that an area of land that might be used to feed, say, ten people on vegetable crops will only feed one person if it's used to feed an animal that's been bred to be eaten.

Fifteen million children will die from malnutrition or related diseases each year, yet the world's cattle alone consume a quantity of food equal to the needs of twice the population of our planet.

If it were not for the developed societies' habit of eating meat, there could be enough vegetable crops grown to feed twice the world's population. Think about it: it's not just animals who die in aid of the Sunday roast – humans die, too.

10 ACRES (5 football pitches)
will support –

61 people
growing SOYA

24 people
growing WHEAT

10 people
growing MAIZE

2 people
growing CATTLE

One acre of land can produce 9000 kg (20,000 lbs) of potatoes but only 70 kg (160 lbs) of beef.

Factory farming

The invention of factory farming has just made things worse. Not only are there thousands more animals to feed, but they are kept inside, so good quality farmland has to be used to grow food for them; whereas, if fewer animals lived outdoors, they would be able to live on lower quality grazing land, leaving the better fields free for growing crops for people.

We buy millions of tonnes of animal food from poor countries because it's cheap to do so. Farmers in under-developed countries like Ethiopia are forced by poverty to use all their best farmland to grow crops for us – rather than growing crops for themselves. It's one of the few means they have to make money.

> Farm animals also consume eighty per cent of world's fresh water.

Third-world loans

When you hear about banks lending money to the developing countries, what you don't hear about are the strict conditions set by the banks, to which the borrowing countries have to agree in order to get the loan. When the rich banks of the West lent money to Costa Rica in the late 1970s, the Costa Rican government had to agree to chop down large areas of rainforest and turn it into grazing land to farm cattle for us. Thousands of peasants were thrown off their land (many were even rumoured to have been murdered) and were left with no means to support themselves.

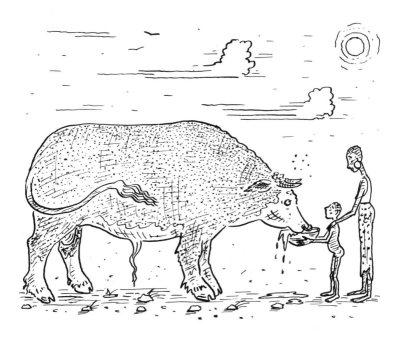

Every time someone in the West eats a take-away burger, they're creating a demand for cheap beef, which means this sort of behaviour on the part of big unscrupulous industries will continue.

The EEC is the largest buyer of animal feed in the world, with 60% coming from starving developing countries.

Destroying the countryside

Today about eighty per cent of British farmland is used for the production of animal produce, either for grazing or growing feed crops. Yet we still have to import food in order to have enough for ourselves.

If we all switched to a vegetarian diet, we could support ourselves on less than twenty-five per cent of the land presently used for farming, without having to resort to using chemicals. We could fertilize the soil with compost, treated human sewage and nitrogenous plants, grown every four years and ploughed back into the ground. The fields could be protected by hedges and trees, which could also be used to produce fruit and nuts. The land no longer needed for farming could be turned into parks, woods and nature reserves.

Unfortunately, this is very unlikely to happen in the near future as it's not in the interests of either the farmers or the government to encourage this idea.

Britain alone could support a population of 250 million people on a vegetarian diet without the use of pesticides.

5

Environmental Reasons for Being Vegetarian

Trees

Trees are vital to the running of the planet. They protect the soil, encourage rainfall, prevent floods, make oxygen and provide homes for all sorts of plants and wildlife. Everyone knows that we can't live without them but people continue to chop them down at an alarming rate.

By now we all know about the threat to the world's rainforests – but do people know why they are being cut down? The main reason isn't to make paper or build furniture – it's to make room for cattle ranching, and for cropland for growing animal feed. The ranchers sow grass in place of the felled trees. The ground and the climate isn't right for growing

grass so after a few years it will die off and the whole area will turn into desert. And more of the forest will have to be destroyed to provide new cropland for cattle.

Two hundred and sixty million acres of forest in the USA have been cleared to make space for the meat industry. In America an acre of trees disappears every eight seconds.

It has been calculated that for every burger eaten, half a tonne of vegetation is lost forever. By switching to a veggie diet you'll be saving about an acre of trees a year.

Tropical rainforests

What is the big deal about rainforests anyway, and why should it matter if they're cut down to make beef-farming land? Well – here are just some facts about what these unique regions give the world:

Oxygen

Air needs to be exactly twenty-one per cent oxygen in order for us to live. Any more and whole countries could be set alight by one stroke of lightning, since things burn much more easily in oxygen-rich atmospheres. Any less and we wouldn't have enough to breathe.

Trees absorb energy from the sun using a process called photosynthesis. They take in carbon dioxide and release oxygen. The right balance of oxygen on this planet depends on trees and plants.

One-third of the world's forest cover is found in the Amazon rainforest area. The trees in the Amazon are especially important as these tropical forest trees photosynthesize at ten times the rate of other trees, which means that they absorb much more carbon dioxide and produce much more oxygen. In fact, the Amazon rainforest is where half the world's oxygen comes from. Without it, we'd be hard pushed to survive. Yet it continues to disappear.

In 1950 one-third of the earth's landmass was covered with tropical forest. By 1975 this figure had shrunk to just over one-fifth, and by 1988 rainforests made up only six per cent of the world's surface.

If we continue cutting at our present rate, by the year 2000 all the forests in Nigeria and the Ivory Coast will have gone; Costa Rica will only have twenty per cent of its forest land left; and Brazil will have lost an area of forest as big as Portugal.

Half the world's rainforests have already been destroyed to make cropland for meat production. If we don't reduce our meat consumption soon, we'll destroy our planet – all for the sake of something that doesn't do us any good anyway.

Forest wildlife

The forests aren't only important for creating oxygen; they also house at least half of all the animal and plant species on earth. Biologists have guessed that there are about 2500 types of tree, 1800 types of bird, 2000 different types of fish and around one million species of plants and animals all living in the rainforests.

At the moment only eight types of plant provide eighty-five per cent of the world's food. If any of these was completely destroyed by disease we would have to go back to the rainforest to look for new strains. If the rainforests were no longer there, we would soon be plunged into starvation.

Medicine

Many of the plants in the rainforests are used in medicine. In fact, twenty-five per cent of conventional drugs come from the tropical forests. Fifteen per cent of Costa Rica's plants have anti-cancer properties, and extracts from a particular type of tree found in the Amazon are being tested as a drug to treat people with AIDS. If we convert the rainforests into vast cattle grounds and cropfields, we lose an extremely important source of natural medicine.

Forest Indians

Another fact that some of us seem to forget is that people actually live in the rainforests. About fifty million tribespeople once lived there but the numbers are decreasing rapidly. In 1900 there were one million Indians in Brazil; now there are only a quarter of a million. During the last ninety years at least one tribe a year has become extinct.

Water pollution

The UK's major source of water pollution is probably from factory farming. A typical battery farm produces over 300,000 kilos of excrement every week. A small pig farm of 2,000 pigs – small by today's standards – will produce 5 tons of urine a day. And where does all this waste go? There is simply too much to return it safely to the land. However it is stored, it inevitably leaks into our reservoirs and rivers, killing fish and polluting our drinking water. In Holland, liquid manure is stored in tanks and then dumped. Ammonia, a blinding acid chemical evaporates from the manure and causes acid rain, which has already destroyed one third of the forests in Holland.

Because herds of animals are so huge these days, many farmers are relying on sileage to feed them – rotted down fermenting grass, stored in high towers. It's more compact to store than fresh hay – and it's deadly to water. Sileage liquor is so poisonous that when it enters a stream it kills all life within.

Many farmers are aware of the problem but simply don't care. They find it more economic to pay the tiny fines imposed for this sort of environmental damage than to sort out the problem.

Four fifths of all agricultural land is now used to feed animals.

Pesticides

Every year *a billion gallons* of pesticides are sprayed on British land alone, to try and support the intensive farming practices the meat habit demands. As we've already pointed out in the health section, these do you no good at all. But they're also dangerous to the environment. Millions of insects, butterflies and moths have been killed or contaminated by pesticides. Animals which eat these insects then take the poisons into *their* bodies and die as well. The barn owl, otter, hare and many birds are all thought to be affected by pesticides.

Topsoil

One reason we need to use so many pesticides and chemicals on our soil is because of the destruction of the topsoil. Topsoil is the rich, dark nutrient-filled soil that lies on the surface. It is essential for growing plants. It is the basic tool for life on earth,

along with water and oxygen (both also under threat from meat eating). The pressure on the land to grow intensive crops for billions of animals is causing us to use up the topsoil faster than it can replenish itself. In the UK almost half the arable (capable of growing crops) land is at risk from soil erosion. The USA has lost almost three quarters of its topsoil. You might argue that any sort of farming would use up the topsoil – but intensive growing of crops for cattle makes 95% more demand on the soil than growing vegetarian food does.

Water

Fresh water is not a resource that is endless – if we use it up faster than it replaces, we'll run out of water. It takes up to 100 times more water to produce one kilo of meat than it does to produce one kilo of wheat.

6

CRUELTY IN OTHER ANIMAL PRODUCTS

Having decided that you don't want to eat meat because you don't like the idea of animals being killed, you may begin to worry about what happens to them down on the farm whilst they're still alive. Meat-eaters often believe that farm animals are allowed to wander around the countryside for a few years before being painlessly put to sleep. Unfortunately, this isn't true.

If you do object to the way they are treated and you don't want to give up animal products completely you can just be more careful about which ones you buy. Health-food shops sometimes stock milk, cheese, eggs and honey made on small farms where the animals are better looked after.

If it had never occurred to you that animals might suffer in the making of things like cheese, yoghurt and butter (not to mention silk and wool), then here is a rough guide to what they have to put up with.

Milk, yoghurt and butter

Although milking doesn't actually hurt a healthy cow, it isn't completely natural for them to carry on producing milk when they no longer have a calf to feed. Just like human mothers, cows produce milk to feed their own offspring. But unlike human

mothers, who stop producing milk when their babies are old enough to eat other things, cows have their calves taken away from them when they aren't really old enough to be weaned, and are forced to carry on producing milk.

This is how it works: while a woman is breastfeeding her child, she continues to produce milk. If the milk is being used, then more will be made. When the baby stops drinking it, the mother stops producing it. Milking a cow is rather like taking away a woman's baby and milking her by machine.

Many people think that a cow will explode if it isn't milked (and it is true that if you suddenly stopped milking a cow that had been bred purely for that purpose, it would take a while to stop lactating and would feel very uncomfortable). But cows aren't natural milk machines any more than women are.

Hormones

In order to raise their milk yields, cows are fed with a hormone, BST which raises the yield by as much as twenty per cent. Cows are also specially bred to create genetically good milk makers. This means that cows are being forced to produce far more milk than they should naturally be able to. Because of this, all the food they eat goes towards making milk rather than feeding themselves. The result is that they gradually waste away and eventually starve to death. The average lifespan of a dairy cow is now only five or six years, whereas it used to be about twenty.

Is it OK to drink cows' milk from a small farm?

Ethical milk production (in big fields without chemicals) seems like a good idea, but it will always be difficult to get milk that hasn't in some way contributed to animal suffering. Take, for example, what happens to bull calves born to dairy cows. They are obviously of no use in a dairy (since males don't produce milk) and while farmers may keep one or two for breeding, the rest have nowhere to go. They cannot be set free or kept as pets, so they are sent to be slaughtered. So it should come as no surprise that about eighty per cent of our beef comes from the dairy industry.

Cheese

Obviously, if the production of milk involves cruelty, then the production of cheese does too. Also most cheese is made with rennet, which is the stomach lining of calves, and is therefore not vegetarian. If cheese is veggie then it will usually say so on the packet. Ricotta, cream cheese and cottage cheese sometimes don't contain rennet but you can never be sure they're safe. So if you plan to be a strict veggie it's worth getting info from The Vegetarian Society about what's OK and what isn't.

Eggs

The eggs you eat are unfertilized, so they are NOT chicken foetuses and could never have hatched and grown into hens. So when you eat an egg you are not eating an animal (or a potential one). As with milk it is not the eggs themselves that are the problem, but what happens to the hens that lay them.

Most eggs (around 90%) are produced on battery farms, where the hens are squashed together in tiny cages. They are extremely uncomfortable as well as bored, which makes them irritable. Their beaks are clipped at birth with a red hot blade to stop them pecking each other to pieces when they grow up.

This is very painful and many of the chicks die. When they are old enough they are put into a cage, where they will probably remain until they die. The cages often have mesh floors so the hens' feet become badly deformed. They are fed by conveyor belt, so diseases spread very quickly, and are given animal waste to eat, some of which is chicken, making them into cannibals. About two million chickens die each year in these conditions.

When hens are too old and exhausted to carry on laying eggs they are slaughtered and sold for cheap meat products like soups and pies, or to pet food manufacturers. No wonder true vegetarians make sure they only do eat free-range eggs.

Free-range eggs

Free-range eggs are from farms where the hens are allowed to wander around, but how much space they have to wander round in depends entirely on the farmer. Free-range egg farms aren't neccessarily the most delightful environment for a hen. Conditions can still be very cramped and the birds can get quite fed up.

Free-range hens are also often fed on slaughterhouse leftovers. Even some eggs sold in health-food shops may have been laid by cannibal hens. The only way to find out what the hens have been eating (if the people in the shop don't know) is by contacting the farmer (the name of the farm will usually be on the box).

Male chicks

It's not only the hens you have to worry about. Because eggs have to be unfertilized, all the male chicks are killed as are older hens. So egg production also involves the slaughter of animals.

Silk

Silk is woven from the threads of the silkworm's cocoon. Some people (including vegetarians) think that silkworms are too small and insignificant to worry about. But, in order to get extra-long threads, some silk manufacturers take the cocoons (with the silkworms still inside) and drop them into boiling water to make the threads unwind.

Wool

Shearing doesn't actually hurt sheep. They do panic a bit but they probably aren't emotionally scarred by the experience. However it's *when* they are sheared that causes problems. Shearing is supposed to be done in the spring. Unfortunately, a lot of British farmers think that spring starts at the beginning of March. This means that the sheep often have to sit through a couple of months of freezing cold weather without any wool to keep them warm. When summer finally comes along their coats have just about grown back and they have to sit and sweat until the weather cools down again.

Australian sheep probably have the worst time of all as many of them are not at all suited to the climate. Not only that, but there is a type of fly that lays its eggs in the skin of the sheep's hind quarters. As the skin flakes off valuable wool is wasted. To prevent flies laying their eggs in the first place, farmers skin the lambs' hind quarters so they remain bald when the skin grows back. Needless to say, this is very painful.

7

HIDDEN NASTIES TO WATCH OUT FOR

It's easy to spot a bit of meat and avoid it, but there are plenty of things made with bits of dead animal that come as a surprise when you go veggie. You would never guess that so many cakes and biscuits that look so sweet and harmless could have such disgusting things in them.

Did you know, for instance, that Polos are made with hooves, horns and bones? Or that margarine often contains animal and fish fat?

Here is a list of the commonest nasty ingredients and where you're likely to find them. If you're planning on being a strict veggie (and no one but you can decide that) you'll need to get into the habit of reading the ingredients on everything. It's a pain at first but it soon becomes instinctive.

E Numbers

E numbers are the serial numbers you find on food labels, telling you which additives the foods contain. It's quite a good idea to get a book or leaflet telling you what the individual E numbers mean. You may actually be surprised to find out how harmless and natural some of them are. Tartaric acid, which is just made from grapes, is sometimes listed as E334. So if you know what they mean you needn't avoid them altogether. There are, however,

quite a few that are worth watching out for, some because they aren't vegetarian and some because they aren't good for you. A good book to get would be *E for Additives* (published by Penguin Books) which you can find in most bookshops or borrow from your library.

Animal Fat

Animal fat does actually mean fat from a dead animal and NOT butter. It turns up all the time in biscuits, cakes and margarine – especially the cheaper brands. The E number E471 also sometimes means animal fat. You often find it in ice cream and dried packet food – i.e. soups and noodles. You can't tell whether it's animal or vegetable just by looking at the ingredients so you can either avoid foods containing E471 altogether or get a list of which products are veggie and which ones aren't. Quite a few supermarkets have started to publish their own.

Cheese (in biscuits and processed food)

Unless it's specifically stated that the cheese is vegetarian, you can pretty well take it for granted that it will have been made with rennet, which is made from calves' stomachs. Many shops and supermarkets now sell vegetarian Cheddar and other brands.

Cochineal

Cochineal is also called E202 and carmine. This red food colouring is made from grubs. You need to watch out for it in sweets, jellies and anything coloured red or pink.

Eggs

Egg is used in all sorts of packaged food – especially biscuits and cakes. You can be quite certain that eggs found in supermarket-bought food (as opposed to food bought in health-food shops) will not be free-range (unless they actually say they are). You could guarantee that any big cake company doing anything as fantastically Green and world-saving as using non-battery eggs would write it all over the packet. So if it doesn't say free-range, it isn't.

Gelatine/glycerol

You find gelatine in sweets, jelly, wine gums, thick and creamy, low fat and set yoghurts, mousses, cheesecakes and quite a few other things. It's made from the boiled up bones, skins, hooves and horns of farm animals (including horses). It is what's known as a slaughterhouse by-product, along with leather, cow gum and certain types of animal food.

Lard

Lots of breads, cakes and pastry contain lard, which is 100 per cent pure animal fat.

Suet

This is chopped-up animal fat found in mincemeat (the sweet kind used in mince pies), Christmas pudding and other baked or steamed puddings, as well as heavy cakes. Vegetarian suet is now widely available.

Vitamins

Vitamins added to foods (especially cereals) are often of animal origin. At the moment only one type of Kelloggs' cereal (Summer Harvest) is completely vegetarian. All the others contain vitamin D3, which is a slaughterhouse by-product.

If there is something that you particularly like that has been fortified with vitamins you could try writing to the manufacturer and asking where they've come from. This not only helps you, it also lets the manufacturer know that people do care about what they're eating.

Lecithin

Lecithin is used a lot in sweets and chocolates. Although it can be found in plants, it can also come from egg yolks, and if so, the eggs will almost certainly not have been free-range.

Quorn or Mycoprotein

This is a relatively new foodstuff which is sold as a meat substitute with a chicken-like texture. It's rich in protein and contains no animal fat and many veggies eat it. *However*, it is made with battery eggs and was tested on animals when it was being developed so it does not have the approval of The Vegetarian Society. Those are the facts: it's up to you whether you eat it or not.

Whey

Whey is a by-product of cheese. Many veggies won't eat it because the cheese it comes from is more than likely to have been made with rennet. Watch out for it in biscuits, cakes, savoury snacks and chocolates.

Worcester sauce

Worcester sauce as made by Lea and Perrins contains anchovy fish. Bottled tomato juice – especially the type you get in pubs – often has Worcester sauce already mixed in. If it's something that you particularly like you can buy vegetarian versions – just read the ingredients lists till you find one that isn't made with anchovies.

This is only a list of some of the most basic and common 'hidden nasties'. The Vegetarian Society (see p. 152) will send you a brilliantly full and comprehensive list called *Vegetarian Stumbling Blocks* if you send an sae. Even better is their book 'The Vegetarian Handbook' which includes a full list of things to watch out for.

8

NUTRITION

Of course becoming a veggie won't make you a picture of health overnight. It's very important to have a properly balanced diet – and that doesn't mean stuffing your face with veggieburgers and chips fried in vegetable oil everyday. However, being a vegetarian doesn't mean that you have to eat mountains of salad and bran either, so don't panic!

Your diet

A varied vegetarian diet will supply all the essential nutrients you need to be fit and healthy – despite what anybody else might tell you. And it'll be a lot healthier for you than the average meat-eater's diet!

Fruit and vegetables; beans and pulses; grains (i.e. rice and breads); and nuts and seeds are the four main food groups within a vegetarian diet. You won't go far wrong if you include something from each of these food groups every day in what you eat.

It's impossible to give full nutritional advice in a short chapter, so look out for veggie books which include recipe ideas and advice on nutrition too. (Sarah Brown's *Vegetarian Cookery* is particularly good, or contact The Vegetarian Society for a list of the books they recommend.) However, this chapter will give you an idea of how to balance your diet properly.

You'll notice some foodstuffs being mentioned again and again – yeast extract (Marmite), green leafy vegetables and nuts, for example – so try to keep them in mind when you're planning meals. Top up with a wholemeal Marmite sandwich or a handful of brazil nuts if you've pigged out on unhealthy food.

Don't try to force yourself to eat foods you really hate because you think they'll be good for you – try to find a substitute that you will enjoy. For example, if the thought of boiled green vegetables (full of calcium and iron by the way!) makes you throw up, then why not try adding them to soup instead, puréeing them into pâté, or throwing them into a stir-fried Chinese meal. If you still can't face the idea, then try to find something else that gives you those nutrients.

Basics

To stay healthy (and alive) you need protein, carbohydrate, fat, sugar, vitamins and minerals. Fat, carbohydrate and sugar tend not to be a problem, apart from the fact that most of us eat too much. The others won't be, either, if you eat a well balanced diet. If you're not entirely sure what a balanced diet entails then here's a guide to what you should be eating and why. If it all seems complicated and confusing, don't worry too much. As long as you eat a good mixture of fresh fruit, different vegetables, beans, grains, nuts and dairy produce (this is the only one that isn't essential) then you'll be fine, if not even healthier than before.

Although looking at vitamin charts may make you wonder, being vegetarian really doesn't mean you have to eat mountains of spinach and bran on a daily basis. There are plenty of veggies who seem to live on a diet of cheese pasties, chips and chocolate, many of whom aren't all that spotty either! But something in between the two is probably what most vegetarians eat.

Protein

We need protein for growth, healing and building new cells. The disease caused by a lack of protein is kwashiorkor. You probably haven't heard of it because virtually no one in the developed countries gets it. The diseases caused by eating too much protein are osteoporosis and kidney failure. The first may sound unfamiliar, but everyone's heard of kidney failure because millions of people suffer from it. The idea that protein deficiency is likely when you give up meat is nonsense.

One of the main dangers when switching to a vegetarian diet is that you will eat tons of cheese and eggs to compensate for the things you may feel you are missing out on by giving up meat. By doing this you'll end up eating almost as much saturated fat, antibiotics and pesticides as you did before. Try to make up the bulk of your protein with nuts, pulses, beans and grains.

Complementary proteins

Protein is made from a complex system of amino acids. We can only use them properly if they are in the right patterns or proportions. We need to get nine of these acids in our food and, using these, our bodies can make the rest. If we don't get enough of one of them, the others are affected. The only foods that contain amino acids in the right – or almost right – proportions are meat, fish, milk, cheese, eggs, soya products and some seaweeds. These foods contain 'complete' proteins.

Vegetable protein sources like beans, nuts and cereals only contain some amino acids so they are known as 'incomplete' proteins. But this doesn't mean that they are inferior.

Beans are high in one type of amino acid (lysine) and low in another (methionine). Rice is the other way round. So if you eat rice and beans together they balance each other out and make a complete protein, which can be better than protein from meat.

Balancing your proteins

Vegetarian protein sources fall into four main groups:

Pulses and beans – Lentils, chick peas, kidney beans, etc, (and peanuts which are, botanically speaking, beans and not nuts).

Grains and cereals – Rice, wheat, flour, oats, corn, bran.

Nuts and seeds – Almonds, brazil nuts, sunflower seeds, sesame seeds, tahini, pine nuts.

Dairy products and eggs – Milk, cheese, yoghurt, fromage frais.

Some combinations are better than others:

Very good combinations

Nuts and seeds combined with pulses and beans as in: Lentil and nut loaf, bean stew topped with sunflower seeds and hummus (chick peas and tahini).

Grains and cereals with pulses and beans as in: Spaghetti with beans, baked beans on toast, peanut butter sandwich, kidney beans and sweetcorn, lentils with rice, soya milk and cereal, oat and peanut flapjacks.

Grains and cereals with dairy products and eggs as in: Rice pudding, cheese on toast, pizza, quiche, cereal and milk, cream cakes, cheese and biscuits and boiled egg and soldiers.

Usually good combinations

Grains and cereals, and nuts and seeds as in: Tahini on toast, nutty biscuits and sesame seeds with rice.

Nuts and seeds with dairy products and eggs as in: Yoghurt and walnuts, and cheese with Brazil nuts.

Beans and pulses with dairy products and eggs as in: Omelette with bean salad, and cheese and lentil slice.

However, if all this sounds horribly complicated, don't get in a sweat. These days nutritionists reckon that you don't have to be so careful with your protein balances in order to get enough protein. If your weekly diet contains a decent range of different foods – and especially protein-rich foods – then they reckon your body balances out the various amino acids for itself over several days.

These aren't the only sources of protein. Protein is also found in potatoes, yeast extract, avocados and most vegetables – especially spinach, asparagus, parsley, broccoli and cabbage.

Vitamins

Vitamin A
You need vitamin A for healthy skin, good eyesight and to help you resist infection. Although you only find it in animal products, it can be made in the body from carotene, which you find in orange and green vegetables and certain fruits. A shortage of vitamin A causes tired eyes and irritability.

Where to find it – Carrots, parsley, spinach, butter, vegetarian cheese, vegetarian/vegan margarine, dried apricots, watercress, broccoli, and mango.

Vitamin B
There are a number of B vitamins. They all do different things but they are grouped together because they have to be in the right proportions to one another to work properly. They're necessary for proper digestion and for the formation of red blood cells.

B1 (thiamin)

Needed to turn carbohydrates into energy. The more bread and potatoes you eat the more vitamin B1 you need.

Where to find it – Marmite, Brazil nuts, peanuts, bran, brown rice, soya flour, wholewheat bread, hazelnuts, peas, beans.

B2 (riboflavin)

Helps your body repair itself. Lack of B2 can cause chapped lips and bloodshot eyes.

Where to find it – Almonds, wholewheat bread, dried peaches, mushrooms, broad beans, dates. The main source for most people is milk, so if you don't drink it make sure you make up for it by eating the right foods or taking the occasional supplement.

B3 (niacin or nicotinic acid)

Deficiency causes irritability, nervousness and depression. Again, dairy products and eggs are the main sources so vegans have to be a bit careful not to miss out.

Where to find it – Marmite, bran, peanuts, wholewheat bread, mushrooms, dried dates and apricots and broad beans.

B6 (pyridoxine)

An anti-stress vitamin which helps regulate the nervous system. Important for women who are on the contraceptive pill, pregnant or suffering from pre-menstrual stress. If you don't get enough you become tired, headachy, depressed and eventually anaemic.

Where to find it – Bran, Marmite, nuts, soya flour, bananas, avocados, cauliflower, green leafy vegetables, root vegetables, dried fruit.

B12

Needed for normal cell division and supplying energy to the muscles. The main vegetarian sources of B12 are milk products and eggs. But if you don't eat them you can buy soya milk and other vegan foods that have been fortified. Lack of B12 can lead to paralysis, anaemia and menstrual problems. You can buy vegetarian and vegan B12 supplements and it is a good idea to do so.

Where to find it – Eggs, vegetarian cheese, Marmite, miso, seaweed, milk and fortified vegan and vegetarian foods.

Folic acid

Helps maintain the metabolic process. Deficiency can lead to anaemia. It is particularly important if you are pregnant. Found in leafy vegetables. Most of it disappears when you cook it so avoid deficiency by eating leafy salads.

Where to find it – Yeast, endive, green leafy vegetables, bran, wheatgerm, nuts, oranges and beans.

Vitamin C (ascorbic acid)

Important in healing, cell structure and for absorbing iron. It helps prevent colds and diseases. Smokers, people on the contraceptive pill or antibiotics, excessive coffee drinkers, drug users and people under stress all need lots of vitamin C. If you don't get enough your gums may start to bleed, you'll be more likely to catch an infection and you'll take ages to get better.

Where to find it – Red pepper, watercress, cabbage, strawberries, cauliflower, oranges, broccoli, raspberries and spinach.

Vitamin D

Your body needs vitamin D in order to absorb calcium and phosphorus. You get it from sunlight and, luckily for people who live in countries like Britain, you don't need very much. Twenty minutes with your face and hands exposed to daylight provides enough for one day.

Where to find it – Sunlight, dairy products, eggs and fortified vegan and vegetarian food (ie foods with added vitamin D).

Vitamin E
Prevents cuts leaving scars. Necessary for cell formation.
Where to find it – Margarine, cereal, eggs, wholemeal bread and nuts.

Minerals

Calcium
Needed for strong teeth and bones, and healthy nerves. The idea that your bones will become weak and brittle due to lack of calcium is a myth. Everyone's bones waste away as they grow older. The average meat-eating woman's bone loss by the age of sixty five will be thirty five per cent. The average vegetarian's will only be fifteen per cent. Lack of calcium can cause irritability, cramps, nervous exhaustion and insomnia.
Where to find it – Vegetarian cheeses, green leafy vegetables, butter, parsley, almonds, watercress, soya, flour, eggs, milk and lemons.

Iron
Important for healthy blood and to transport oxygen around the body. If you eat plenty of vitamin C your body will find it easier to absorb iron. Not enough iron in the diet leads to lethargy and anaemia.
Where to find it – Bran, wheatgerm, parsley, soya flour, millet, yeast, dried fruit, green vegetables and Marmite.

Sodium and potassium
Sodium just means salt, and most of us get too much rather than too little. Potassium is found in all sorts of food, but it is destroyed when food is overcooked. Deficiency can cause heart attacks so make sure you eat plenty of fresh fruit and not too much salt, as salt prevents the digestion of potassium.
Where to find it – Marmite, dried fruit, soya flour, almonds, brazil nuts, molasses and parsley.

Magnesium

Needed to make some of the other vitamins and minerals work properly. Lack of it causes cramps, especially at night, and nervous depression. Too many soft drinks, sweets and alcohol can also cause a deficiency.

Where to find it – Bran, Brazil nuts, almonds, soya flour, chick peas, spinach, dried apricots, peanuts, oats, wholewheat bread and wheatgerm.

Zinc

Nobody knows exactly what it's for but if you don't get enough you may suffer from infertility and slow healing of wounds. The amount of zinc in food depends mainly on the amount of zinc in the soil it was grown in.

There are a few other vitamins and minerals, such as phosphorus, iodine and vitamin K, which are all very easily available in all sorts of food so you don't need to think about whether or not you're getting enough.

9

WEIRD AND WONDERFUL INGREDIENTS

Vegetarian recipe books are full of weird and wonderful ingredients that the average meat-eater has either never heard of or never uses. Here are some that you may have come across, with hints on what to do with them.

Agar-agar

Agar-agar is a very useful ingredient and the vegetarian alternative to animal gelatine. It's made from different seaweeds, rather than boiled bones. It makes reasonable tasting jelly using real fruit juice and fruit pieces. It has a slightly more grainy texture than normal jelly and can taste a bit salty; otherwise it's not a bad replacement.

Beans

Beans are one of the most versatile foodstuffs around. Health-food shops are stacked with all sorts of different types of beans – so you'll never get bored of experimenting with them. You can mash them up to make burgers, loaves and pâtés, leave them whole in sauces or stews or put them in salads. Not only are beans a fantastic source of protein but they're chock full of minerals like zinc and iron, as well as calcium, vitamins A and C and, of course, good old fibre. Their health-giving qualities have been recognized for centuries – hence the expression 'full of beans'.

Do read labels on dried beans carefully as various types need different preparation and cooking times.

Aduki beans are a type of kidney bean, mainly grown in China and Japan. They're small with a nutty taste and are a great addition to stews and soups.

Black-eyed beans These are handy because, like lentils, they don't need overnight soaking, and cook in about thirty minutes. Great for a quick veg curry!

Broad beans are nicest eaten fresh and make a delicious accompaniment to main meals. They are also available in cans and as dried beans.

Butter/Lima beans are quite large, creamy coloured and have a soft texture. Chuck them in soups and stews and use them puréed in pâtés.

Chick peas are golden coloured and have a scrummy nutty flavour. They're available either dried or canned. Chick peas are used in Middle-Eastern dishes like hummus, a tasty garlicky dip, and falafels, which are deep-fried patties made with spices and onion.

Flageolet beans – Pale green kidney beans with a delicate flavour.

Haricot beans are probably best known to everyone as baked beans. These amazing beans contain more protein than meat!

Kidney beans are a variety of runner bean and are usually used in spicy Mexican dishes like chilli.

Mung beans are small and green and in their sprouted form known as bean sprouts – perfect for stir-fries and salads.

Lentils

Lentils are low in fat and high in fibre. They can be green, red, orange, yellow or brown and are available as whole beans or split. Try making spaghetti sauces or shepherd's pie using lentils, or experiment with them in Indian dishes.

Carob

Carob is a chocolate alternative. On its own it doesn't taste that brilliant but it's OK in cakes and biscuits. Try making chocolate brownies or cookies with it – it's caffeine free, unlike chocolate.

Dried fruits

Dried fruits, particularly apricots and figs, contain loads of minerals and vitamins, including iron. They can be high in calories as they're so sweet, but console yourself with the knowledge that the sugar is natural, unlike the sugar in chocolate. Try chopping some dried fruit into a salad or having it on cereal.

Flours

Flour is useful for binding things like homemade burgers. It helps them to hold their shape and not crumble. Gram flour, which is made from chick peas, is especially good for this. One tablespoon of gram flour and one of water can be used to replace the egg in loaf and burger mixes.

Health-food shops tend to stock a variety of different types of flour. Buckwheat flour makes good muffins and pancakes; soya flour contains lecithin, like eggs, so it can be used to bind things in the same way as gram flour or to make vegan pancakes and batter; and rice flour makes crunchy biscuits.

Grains

Many vegetarians seem to base around eighty per cent of their meals on rice or pasta. They're great convenience foods and really good for you – especially if you use the wholemeal kinds. But there are lots of other types of grains you may enjoy trying. They're all packed with nutrients and many take less than ten minutes to cook.

Wholewheat is like chewy brown rice.
Whole barley grains (or berries) are similar. Both make a great base for salads.

Cous-cous, also called bulghar wheat or cracked wheat, is really easy to cook and only takes about seven minutes. It's very yummy and great for absorbing flavours – try it with a mushroom sauce. It's also the basis for a great Middle-Eastern salad, tabbouleh, where the grain is used to soak up oil and lemon mixed with chopped parsley, onion and tomato. Try it in a range of salads and stuffings.

Rye has a striking flavour and can be used as a replacement for rice.

Millet has a dry consistency and is another grain that's easy to cook.

Herbs

You don't have to limit yourself to salt and pepper – herbs are guaranteed to tickle your taste buds and liven up the most boring of dishes. And if you're green-fingered, many are easy to grow at home, in the garden or on a windowsill.

Basil, dried or fresh, is great in tomato dishes.

Chives, a member of the onion family, will zap up egg dishes, like omelettes, or give extra zing to salads.

Marjoram peps up cheese or egg dishes.

Oregano does wonders for Italian-type dishes, particularly pizzas and pasta sauces.

Parsley adds zest to any stews, soups, salads or sauces, and is full of minerals too.

Rosemary, fresh or dried, is a nice addition to soups or stews and casseroles. It has quite a strong flavour and can also be added to sauces and egg dishes.

Thyme goes well with egg dishes, too, and is a great flavourer for rice.

Spices

Spices cost next to nothing and can be the making of a vegetarian meal. Try to find a shop that sells them by the gram from big jars, rather than investing in a whole range of expensive bottles from the supermarket. Buy a little of each and experiment until you find your favourites. All the Eastern spices are great for zapping up veggie dishes.

Ground cumin, garam masala or *fried cumin seeds* give dishes an authentic curry taste. Cumin will pep up all types of savoury dishes (especially if you grill it first) but beware of eating too much of it as the smell has a nasty habit of coming out through your armpits! A good curry powder can boost all sorts of dishes, from scrambled eggs to baked beans. It's full of iron and very good for you, too.

Turmeric is great for colouring rice a bright yellow, which looks most impressive.

Mixed spice or *cinnamon* can give an intriguing sweetness to savoury dishes like rice.

Cayenne, paprika or *chilli powder* adds a bit of heat to pasta or bean dishes.

Mustard seeds add a crunchy, hot element to creamy, bland dishes like mashed potatoes. And mustard powder will perk up cheese dishes and give them added zing! The great thing about mustard is that it comes in all sorts of flavours and textures.

Ginger, fresh (peeled or grated) or powdered, is great in soups or with carrots or stir-frys.

Nutmeg grated and gently sprinkled over cabbage or spinach really alters the flavour.

Cardamom pods dropped in rice water gives rice a lovely tangy flavour.

Bay leaves (just add one per recipe) are great for dropping into sauces while they simmer – but do remember to take them out before you serve as they taste disgusting on their own.

Keep experimenting – you'll get a few awful tastes somewhere along the way, but you'll discover lots more great ones. And remember, you can always smother any disasters in tomato ketchup to hide the taste.

Mayo/Egg-free mayonnaise

If you give up eggs you can still have egg-free mayonnaise. It's a good idea for egg-eating veggies to eat it too, as ordinary mayonnaise is made with raw battery eggs – and if you're at all aware of the diseases spread in battery farms then you'll know that raw eggs are the worst culprits of all.

If you eat packed lunches, a delicious layer of mayo in your sandwiches is much tastier than margarine any day.

Miso

Miso is the sort of thing that most veggies buy and then leave at the back of the cupboard for two years. But if you remember to use it, it's quite a good thing to have around (especially for vegans). It's a sauce made from cooked soya beans which have been left to ferment for between eighteen months and three years. It's full of protein and all the essential amino acids, calcium and enzymes to help digestion. It's also a very good source of vitamin B12. You can use it instead of stock in soups or as a way of adding flavour and salt to stews and sauces.

Nuts

Nuts are full of protein and minerals. Try to get untreated nuts, especially the ones in their shells, and roast them yourself in the oven or under the grill. Put them on top of things that need baking or in salads and loaves. They're an easy way of grabbing a bit of extra protein. Keep a jar of peanut or cashew butter around for a quick protein top up.

Nuts are very useful for complementing proteins from other food groups, but remember that peanuts are pulses, so mixing peanuts and lentils would be no good. If you, or whoever pays for your food, can afford it, try lots of different nuts. Pecan and macadamia nuts are delicious, like very nice walnuts. Flaked almonds can be scattered on top of almost anything and browned, and go a long way for your money. Pine kernels are expensive but also go a long way and have a delicious flavour.

Seaweed

In Norway there is an institute devoted entirely to Seaweed Research. There they've discovered that seaweed can contain thirteen vitamins, twenty amino acids and sixty trace elements. It's also full of iodine which speeds up your metabolism and can help you lose weight.

Eating seaweed may sound a bit disgusting but it really isn't at all. It's not that easy to buy but if you find a source nearby it's well worth a try. The best one to start with is probably arame. It looks a bit like baby eels but it tastes really good, especially with soy sauce and carrots. Try your local health-food shop, which will probably stock some sorts of seaweed.

Seeds

Seeds are rich in vitamins, minerals, protein and oil. The seeds we eat fall into two main categories: spice seeds and food seeds. Spice seeds are things like cumin, coriander, caraway and poppy seeds. You only use these in very small amounts to add flavour to food, so they're not really suitable for use as a complementary protein (except maybe poppy seeds).

Food seeds are things like pumpkin, sunflower and sesame seeds. They're good for putting in biscuits and salads and on top of things that need to be baked in the oven.

Both sorts of seed are tastier if you cook them first in an un-oiled frying pan or by toasting them quickly under the grill or in a microwave.

Smokey snaps

Smokey snaps are little smokey bacon-flavoured bits of soya. They are vegetarian (or vegan), as are most smokey bacon crisps and snacks. You can sprinkle them on salads, rice, stews or in fact almost anything savoury.

Soya milk

Soya milk is what vegans use instead of cows' milk. It's also good for people who don't want to consume too much fat. It tastes a bit peculiar at first but you soon get used to it and even start to like it. There is almost nothing you can't do with it. You can make milkshakes, white sauces, ice cream and creamy soups and obviously you can put it on cereal and in tea and coffee – but you do have to put quite a lot in coffee as the heat and acidity make small amounts curdle.

You can buy soya milk sweetened or unsweetened. The sweet stuff is more sugary than cows' milk and the unsweetened is less, because cows' milk naturally contains a sugar called lactose.

Soya yoghurt and cheese

Soya yoghurt can be delicious if you get a good brand and quite disgusting if you don't. Some taste just like thick and creamy yoghurts and some are just sickly and curdled. You just have to try a couple until you find one you like.

Soya cheese is a pretty good replacement for cheese in dishes that need cheese on top or a cheesy sauce. But if you really like cheese on its own the soya version will be a bit of a poor substitute. Most soya cheeses tend to be a lot like mozzarella. You can get them with added herbs, garlic or pepper to make them taste a bit less bland.

Tahini

Tahini is a paste made from ground-up sesame seeds. Most people just use it to make hummus, but it's nice on toast with honey or mixed with lemon juice and garlic to make salad dressing.

Tempeh

Tempeh is glutinous stuff made from wheat flour and is a sort of meat substitute.

Tofu

Tofu (also spelt toyfu) is soya bean curd. It's very high in protein and very low in fat. Straight from the packet, its texture is not unlike very soft, spongy rubber. Some people like it just as it is. If you're one of those, you can chop it into salads or drop it into stir-fries or stew. There are also quite a few people who find it completely repulsive in its original state because it is designed to be bland to absorb flavours, but use it well disguised in their cooking. You can blend it with olives, garlic and herbs to make pâté, mash it with rice and onions and fry it to make rissoles, chop it into sticks and fry it to make tofu chips or (if you really hate it but feel determined to eat it because it's good for you) you can mash it with potato and almost pretend it's not there. It comes in three flavours – original, savoury and marinated. If you want to find out how good it can be try it in a dish at a Chinese restaurant – they know how to use it so it will be delicious.

TVP (Textured Vegetable Protein)

TVP is designed to be a meat replacement, so it comes in granules that are supposed to look like minced meat, or meat chunks. You can buy it dried in health-food shops. Although many people use it, TVP is a strange phenomenon – it's not enough like meat to satisfy a meat-loving vegetarian, and it's a bit too much like meat to appeal to a veggie purist. After all, if you hate the idea of cut-up animals, why would you want to eat something that looks just like it?

Vegetable Stock

You can buy vegetable stock cubes in most supermarkets. They tend to be quite salty so if you use one you needn't add salt when you're cooking. You can also buy it in jars. It's often made partly with yeast so it contains lots of good protein and B vitamins.

Part Two

PRACTICE

PRACTICALITIES

OK – you've decided you want to turn veggie; you've learned all the reasons why it's such a good idea; you've swotted up on nutrition and your mind's made up. Now you have to fit vegetarianism into your daily life. Fortunately, it's never been easier to do so. Restaurants, schools, supermarkets and takeaways are all very aware these days of the ever-increasing numbers of vegetarians in Britain – and cater for them accordingly. With almost four million people who describe themselves as vegetarian in the UK and 28,000 people becoming veggie every *week* you've put yourself in good company by choosing the sensible option. And, unless you're very unlucky, you shouldn't have any trouble at home either. In a recent survey carried out among 2,500 11–18 year-olds, only 5% experienced real difficulties being vegetarian, and 67% said their parents were really helpful or didn't mind at all. Maybe in the past vegetarians encountered prejudice from some meat eaters – but these days it's recognized to be such a sane and common decision that it's now the diehard and selfish carnivores who are taking the stick.

10

FAMILY

We all know that families can be a real pain at times and often a new lifestyle can send them completely potty! If you are unlucky enough to hit a negative reaction, here are some of the commonest:

'We won't have that sort of nonsense in this family . . .'

The main reason for this sort of announcement is that they think *your* eating habits are going to cause *them* lots of aggro. It's important that you don't start off by expecting them to cook for you *or* to pay for lots of extra food for you to cook for yourself. Learn how to adapt the family meals and make use of the food that's around in the house. Explain to them that being vegetarian needn't mean spending hours cooking nut roast *or* spending a fortune on fancy ingredients from health-food shops. Baked beans and spaghetti hoops are as veggie as anything, and healthy too, and no parent is going to claim *they're* hard to cook.

'Vegetarianism isn't logical'

Make sure you've got facts at your fingertips for this one. There's nothing worse than having snotty sisters and brothers winding you up about what you're doing. For some reason people seem to love taking vegetarians on (maybe they feel guilty about eating meat) and giving them counter-arguments. If that's the sort of approach your family takes, read Chapter One of this book thoroughly and stand by to take on all comers with the

sheer sense of your decision – but try not to start arguments yourself just as the family's tucking into its Sunday roast or you will be unpopular.

'But, love, you need to eat meat . . .'

Parents can make a real fuss, so be prepared. They probably think you'll turn a ghastly shade of green and drop dead if you don't get your sausage a day. Swot up on nutrition – that's bound to impress them – then take the trouble to explain what you've learned to your family and convince them that you're not about to fade away.

Don't start scoffing mounds of junk food in front of them – let them see that you're eating properly. Who knows? You may find you can convert the whole family!

'While you're in my house, you'll eat what I give you . . .'

You may find that your family will keep feeding you meat in the vague hope that if they can starve you into submission you'll actually give up trying to be veggie. Basically, you've got two choices. You could just ignore the meat on your plate for a while until they eventually realize that you aren't going to eat it and that they'll have to serve you something you *will* eat. Or you can sit down with them and have a chat about your reasons for wanting to be veggie – without throwing a wobbler!

'Ah, isn't that sweet . . . you don't like eating little animals.'

Often, parents think you're going through an animal-loving phase, one that you'll probably grow out of. Prove to them that it's no phase! They'll soon give up teasing you about it.

Some famous vegetarians who actually ate meat . . .
There are rumours about Hitler, Mussolini and a few other nasty people being veggie. There are even people who ponder for hours and write things about why so many dictators and murderers don't eat meat. This is really a bit of a waste of time as both Hitler and Mussolini actually did. Hitler was put on a vegetarian diet every so often by his doctor to see if it helped his flatulence (he farted a lot, particularly when he was angry, which seems to have been most of the time). His views on animal rights were about as charming as his views on human rights. He wanted to breed animals to create the perfect meat producer in much the same way as he wanted to breed perfect humans.

Shopping

Most supermarkets these days are very aware of vegetarian needs. Even small high-street branches tend to stock a good few veggie dishes, vegetarian cheese, free-range eggs and veggieburgers. It's not a bad idea to go along with whoever does the weekly shop in your house and share the shopping. This has several advantages:

★ You get to show you're taking responsibility for your choices;
★ You can get to have a say in what sort of food you'll end up eating;
★ You're supporting the food buyer/cooker and sharing the work;
★ You can read the ingredients on what's bought and check whether it's OK for you;
★ You can check out new types of veggie food that you might not have thought of.

Keep it simple

At first, at least, it's probably a good idea if you don't start demanding the massively pricey and ready-prepared exotic mushrooms in cream and wine sauce – even if it is only the cost of your share of the Sunday joint. Parents never like it when your ethical choices end up involving extra expense for them, so THINK SIMPLE.

These foods are readily available in virtually any supermarket, and are all fully vegetarian:
Spaghetti hoops
Veggieburgers (usually cost about the same as hamburgers)
Baked beans
Curried baked beans
Tinned kidney beans, butter beans, chickpeas etc – good for salads and meat substitutes
Ready-made pizzas and pizza bases (check for ham and anchovies!)
Pot Noodles

Spicy rice and noodle packets (jazz up with a few peanuts)
Ratatouille (tinned)
Tomato soup
Ready-mixed salads
Veggie bakes
Quiche
Veggie pasties
Crispy pancakes

If you have a freezer at home, then it's worth buying one large pack of veggie grills, for example, which you can pull out every time the rest of the family is having fish fingers – they'll seem to cost more at first, but they'll last much longer than the pack that all the family's tucking into.

Lard/veggie cheese/free-range egg dilemmas

If your parent always cooks with lard or balks at paying extra for free-range eggs or veggie cheese, and this is something that you care about, then you have a problem. Basically, you have two choices:

★ Offer to pay the difference in price out of your own money, explaining that otherwise it will limit your choice and it means a lot to you not to have to eat these things.

★ Or, if they won't budge, and you don't want to compromise, quietly and tactfully engineer meals so you end up never eating their eggs or cheese. This will probably involve you offering to take over responsibility for your own meals. (Take the 'I think it's only fair to you that I handle my own food' line and they'll think how mature you are.)

Shopping for pet foods

You can give dogs a vegetarian diet but not cats. Vegetarian dogs can be perfectly happy, but even so they do seem naturally to prefer meat, and you may discover that your 'vegetarian' dog has been nipping round to the neighbour's for the odd sausage or bone.

If you haven't got a pet but you're thinking about getting one, it might be a good idea to consider animals that are natural herbivores, like hamsters or rabbits.

It's much better not to buy animals from pet shops. Try, instead, to get them from animal homes or from friends.

Sorting out the cooking

Most parents, you may be pleased to hear, are happy to go on cooking for a vegetarian son or daughter and many will really enjoy the challenge (who knows? the whole family may convert thanks to you). But you shouldn't expect them to do all the hard work of thinking up what to cook. If you can be on hand to make useful suggestions for easy trouble-free meals for veggies, you'll be a lot more popular. It shouldn't be hard. There are just as many vegetarian convenience foods as there are meaty ones and you should find it really easy to adapt family meals to suit your needs. If your family is a real meat-and-two-veg one, then you could always eat the veg and potatoes (without gravy) and have some nuts or grated cheese sprinkled over the vegetables to supply your protein. But there are loads of other dishes that can be adapted as well:

Family meals to adapt

Omelette – If the others want to have ham or non-veggie cheese versions, then keep some of the egg mixture separate and either cook it in another pan or cook it first and keep it warm in the oven.
Pasta with tuna or meat – Add beans instead, for protein.

Spaghetti bolognese – Cook your sauce with TVP or just tomatoes (see p. 91 for recipe)

Pizza – Add loads of your favourite toppings to the pizza base.

Sausages or *toad-in-the-hole* – Buy or prepare some veggie sausages and adapt any recipe from there.

Curry – Start off with a big vegetable curry – and let the meat-eaters throw in what they fancy at the end.

Stuffed pancakes – Your family has meat fillings, you have veggie.

Sunday lunch – if there's stuffing, ask for a bit cooked separately for you (if you like it!) and enjoy that plus sauces and the vegetables. Sprinkle some cheese over your vegetables for extra protein.

Burgers or hot dogs – Use veggieburgers or sausages, and then share all those great relishes!

Shepherd's pie, fish pie, lasagne, moussaka – Grab a bit of the mashed potato or white sauce and create a veggie version in a one-person dish using cooked lentils and veg instead of meat.

Chilli con carne – Wap some extra beans into your plate and miss out the meat altogether.

If and when you do eat together as a family, you need to make sure that the vegetables or gravy, or whatever you're going to have, hasn't been made with meat stock or cooked in animal fat. Hopefully, this shouldn't be too much of a problem since vegetarian stock cubes and non-animal fat are readily available. If whoever's cooking insists on using meat stock, then you'll have to make your own sauce alongside, using a vegetable stock cube.

Cooking for yourself

While it's a good idea to start off being veggie gently, by adapting the family meals, it's not a bad idea to learn a bit of cooking – after all, at some point you'll be moving away from home and will need to know how.

What, me cook?!

OK, so the idea of you actually cooking your own meals may freak your family out as much as it freaks you. But you have to learn to cook some time, so you might as well start now.

Get a simple veggie recipe book (there are loads of good ones around). If you follow the instructions with care then there shouldn't be too much mess. But do be careful to clean up afterwards or you'll never be allowed in the kitchen again.

It's fun with one

One great advantage of cooking for yourself is that you can eat whatever you like and avoid the grub you really detest. And, if you get cravings for odd food combinations, like brussels sprouts with chilli sauce, or mashed potato with Marmite, you can tuck in to your heart's content without worrying about anybody else.

You can also rest assured that no one will have contaminated your food with a meaty spoon or added any animal derivatives to it.

If you really get into cooking, you could offer to cook the family meal one night a week – that way you can introduce them to the delights of vegetarian cooking and a whole new range of exciting tastes. If you manage to convert them all, you're really laughing – but even getting them into non-meat once a week is still helping save animals' lives *and* improving your family's health.

If your family shows signs of being a little freaked out by the idea of a veggie meal (some weirdos are) then cook something nice and safe, like macaroni cheese or veggie bolognese that is based on a traditional dish.

Whatever you do, don't give them something unfamiliar like tofu or TVP – you may scare them off forever.

It will be a great advantage for you if you can get the family into veggie food, even if it's only a couple of meat-free meals a week. You may find you'll be cooking more ambitious dishes – with *their* help!

Labour-saving cooking

You'll start to acquire special skills when you make meals for one, like cooking whole dinners and only dirtying one saucepan – great wheeze! Some great washing-up-free meals include pasta and tomato sauce (two saucepans), pizza and salad (a baking tray and a chopping board), baked potato and ratatouille (one saucepan), and soup with cheese on toast (one saucepan, and remember not to let the cheese drip onto the grill!).

You can also create less mess and ultimately less work for yourself by steaming your vegetables in a sieve on top of another pan containing rice or potatoes. This will also use less gas or electricity.

11
RECIPES
FOR HOME

Breakfast

Unless your family regularly tucks into greasy fry-ups in the morning, you probably won't have to change your breakfast habits too drastically. However, you may have to be careful about which cereals you eat as very few are strictly vegetarian (see p. 53). Many contain added vitamin D3 which can come from a slaughterhouse by-product. (The Vegetarian Society can help you learn which are safe.) Alternatively, you could buy a plain cereal base from a health-food shop and add your own nuts and dried fruit and anything else that takes your fancy.

Cereal with yoghurt and fruit

Pour yoghurt (soya yoghurt, if you prefer) on your cereal instead of milk and heap some fresh fruit on top. It tastes absolutely gorgeous and is very filling, too, so you won't be snacking all morning.

Poached eggs on toast with Marmite

It's not a good idea to eat too many eggs, but if you like them this is a delicious and nutritious way of eating them. Simply poach the free-range egg in a poacher or an ordinary pan with simmering water, put it on a piece of toast spread with Marmite and grind some black pepper on top.

Homemade crunchy muesli

Soak some jumbo oats (available in health-food shops) in apple juice mixed with a dollop of honey, until all the juice has been absorbed (this should take a few hours, or leave to soak overnight). Add some nuts and seeds to the mixture (hazelnut, Brazil nuts, unsalted peanuts, sesame seeds or sunflower seeds, for example). Then bake in a moderate oven on a lightly greased baking tray until it goes crunchy (this should take about forty minutes – don't let it get too brown). Break the mixture up, leave it to cool and then add a few bits of dried fruit, if you like. Keep in a tightly-sealed container.

Main Meals

Here are three simple and delicious veggie meals. They're healthy, very easy to make and the ingredients can be adapted to suit whatever is in the fridge.

Stir-fry (for two)

Ingredients

150g (5oz) rice	50g (2oz) peas
1 onion	75g (3oz) cauliflower
1 carrot	50g (2oz) sweetcorn
¼ red or green pepper	1 tablespoon vegetable oil
50g (2oz) green beans	Soy sauce

Optional: fresh ginger (grated and fried) water chestnuts, peanuts and chilli sauce.

1. Put the rice in a saucepan and cook it according to the instructions on the packet (different types of rice take different times to cook). Instead of cooking the rice in water, you could cook it in vegetable stock which gives it a better flavour.
2. Whilst the rice is cooking, chop the onion, carrots and pepper into thin slivers.
3. Top and tail the beans and break the cauliflower into bite sized bits.
4. Measure out the peas and sweetcorn.
5. Drain the rice when it's ready.
6. Put the onions and oil in a frying pan over a medium heat and stir with a wooden spoon until the onions look transparent.
7. Add the rest of the vegetables and a good splash of soy sauce and cook, stirring with a wooden spoon, for about two minutes.
8. Add the rice and cook until it's all heated through.
9. Serve with more soy sauce.

Don't feel you must stick to these ingredients – you can use whatever vegetables are in the fridge or freezer. Mushrooms, bean sprouts, thinly shredded cabbage or courgettes are all good.

Pasta with tomato sauce

Don't buy egg pasta – the eggs won't be free range. Check the packet when you buy it to make sure it hasn't got eggs in. This is the most basic version but you can add things to it. As it is, pasta is the only protein-rich food in the recipe, so put some beans or chickpeas in the sauce, or throw some nuts or cheese on afterwards. Serve with a salad.

Ingredients

1 onion	salt
1 tablespoon vegetable oil	175g (6oz) green or white
1 clove garlic	pasta (egg-free)
1 tin tomatoes	Pepper
1 heaped teaspoon tomato purée	

Optional: fresh or dried rosemary or oregano for flavouring.

1. Chop the onion and fry in oil in a large saucepan over a moderate heat until soft.
2. Crush the garlic and add to the pan.
3. Pour in the tomatoes and break them up with a wooden spoon.
4. Add the tomato purée and herbs (optional) and leave on a low heat to simmer.
5. Put a pan of salted water on to boil. When it boils, add the pasta and maybe a little bit of vegetable oil to stop it sticking together.
6. Simmer for 9–12 minutes (until the pasta's soft), then drain.
7. Taste the sauce to see if it needs any salt or pepper. Add however much you like, then serve it up on top of the pasta.

The longer you can leave it, the better it will taste but the quick version will be done as soon as the pasta's cooked.

Variations
★ Sprinkle some chopped fresh parsley on top.
★ Put a bay leaf in the sauce while it's cooking.
★ Add some tinned kidney beans to the sauce one minute before you serve up.
★ Toss the pasta in olive oil, crushed garlic, poppy seeds or fresh herbs after you've drained it.
★ Add 100g (4oz) of red lentils and half a pint of water to the tomatoes at stage 4. Simmer for an extra fifteen minutes before putting the pasta water on.
★ Add soya mince to the sauce at stage 4.

'Everything' salad

Ingredients
(Choose whatever you like from:)

Rice or pasta	Spring onions
Green or red pepper	Sunflower seeds
Diced cheese	Cauliflower
Nuts	Lightly cooked broccoli
Lettuce	Fruit
Radishes	Cucumber
Sweetcorn	Avocado
Mushrooms	Apples
Fresh herbs	Anything else you can think of

1. If you are having rice or pasta, cook it and cool it by putting it in a sieve and running cold water through it.
2. Prepare and chop the vegetables, leaving any things like apples and avocados until last, to stop them going brown.
3. Toss it all in your favourite dressing, eg mayonnaise, french dressing or lemon juice and olive oil.

As long as you include food from at least two protein groups this will be substantial enough to make a whole meal.

Christmas dinner

Christmas dinner can be rather exciting if you are vegetarian. Instead of having to stick to the same old boring meal you've had every year for the whole of your life, suddenly your options are wide open. You can choose an exciting dish that genuinely is a treat. Read around in cookery books, check out ready-made dishes in up-market shops and find something really tasty. Make sure all the nice extras – like cranberry sauce and stuffing – are veggie or that a bit is cooked separately for you. That way you can enjoy all the trimmings (and let's face it, they're much the nicest bit) *and* have your own specially chosen main course – the others will be green with envy.

Lentil and Brazil nut loaf

You can buy quite nice nut roast mixtures in health-food shops, but homemade ones are definitely better. If you don't want to cook on Christmas day, you could make the mixture a couple of days beforehand and keep it in the freezer. There's nothing difficult about this recipe, there are just lots of different easy things to do. If you're not that accomplished in the kitchen try to persuade someone to give you a hand.

Ingredients

100g (4oz) red lentils	50g (2oz) hard cheese
½ pint cider, wine	50g (2 oz) Brazil nuts
or vegetable stock	fresh or dried herbs
1 small onion	salt and pepper
1 carrot	1 teaspoon margarine
1 stick of celery	25g (1 oz) breadcrumbs
2 tablespoons vegetable oil	1 free range egg

1. Put the lentils and liquid in a saucepan, bring to the boil, then cover and simmer over a low heat for twenty-five minutes, until the liquid has been completely absorbed and the lentils have turned to a smooth, thick paste.

2. Meanwhile, finely chop the onion, carrot and celery and fry them in the vegetable oil until the onion becomes transparent and the vegetables are slightly soft.
3. Grate the cheese.
4. Put the nuts in a bag and bash them with a rolling pin to break them into little bits.
5. Mix the lentils, vegetables, cheese and nuts together.
6. Add salt, pepper and herbs.
7. Grease a loaf tin with the margarine. Tip in the breadcrumbs and give the tin a shake so they stick to the sides.
8. Add the egg to the lentil mixture and stir in very thoroughly.
9. Pour the mixture into the loaf tin and bake in a moderate oven (180°C/Gas mark 5) for thirty-five minutes.

NB If you want to freeze the mixture, rather than cook it at once, let it thaw for a few hours before baking it.

Christmas pudding

You could ask your family to make the pudding with vegetable suet, or buy one from a health-food shop. If neither of these is possible you can make your own delicious chocolate Christmas pudding.

Ingredients
25 g (1 oz) margarine
1 tablespoon set honey
40 g (1½ oz) your favourite biscuits
1 tablespoon icing sugar
25 g (1 oz) mixed fruit
25 g (1 oz) whole nuts
1 tablespoon fruit juice (or use alcohol if you prefer)
100 g (4 oz) bar plain chocolate

1. Put the fruit and nuts in a bowl with the fruit juice. Leave to soak for a couple of hours, stirring every so often.
2. Melt the chocolate, margarine and honey in a saucepan over a very low heat. As soon as the chocolate has melted take

the pan off the heat and add the fruit and nuts, mixing them in well.

3. Bash the biscuits with a rolling pin so they break into different sized bits, then stir into the chocolate mixture.
4. Pour the mixture into a lightly greased, round-bottomed pudding bowl and place in the fridge.
5. Leave it for a good few hours, until it's completely cold, then turn it out on to a plate. Dust with a sprinkling of icing sugar just before you eat it.

Good buys

If you really can't be bothered with heavy-duty cooking, then grab hold of a copy of *The Junk Food Vegetarian* by Jonathan Cainer, published by Piatkus Books. It's an absolute must and a great giggle, too. It's ideal for anyone who wants to be veggie but can't get through the day without a frozen pizza or food straight from the tin!

Of course there are plenty of sensible recipe books available, for example, *Linda McCartney's Home Cooking*, published by Bloomsbury. Even if you don't fancy being a particularly serious cook veggie recipe books are certainly worth checking out if only to learn more about nutrition, and give better suggestions to the cook in your house.

12

Stupid Questions People Ask

'Won't you get really sickly and thin?'

This is a particularly stupid question – after all, who wants to be sickly and thin? If you eat a properly balanced veggie diet, you'll end up being healthier than you were before. The idea that meat = strength is hopelessly old-fashioned and, quite simply, wrong.

Many people who cut out meat and opt for health food do discover that they've lost a little weight, simply because their diet has become healthier and more satisfying. Most people can afford to lose a bit of weight, anyway, but no veggie *has* to. OK, veggies aren't normally regarded as fatties, but there's still plenty of opportunity for chip-eating, Coke-drinking and chocolate-munching sessions; and after all, nuts and avocados – things that veggies are encouraged to eat – are among the highest-protein, highest-calorie foods you can eat!

'Even if you are vegetarian, shouldn't you give your children meat?'

Maybe you're not planning to start a family just yet, but this is a very important topic and one which you'll probably have to think about some time.

There is no evidence to suggest that children suffer either mentally or physically from growing up on a vegetarian diet. In fact, there quite a few second- and third-generation veggie children around to prove that you don't need meat to grow up fit and healthy.

'Don't you get fed up with just eating vegetables?'

Can you believe these questions – they get worse! Some people have this crazy idea that being vegetarian means eating tons of raw or boiled veg. They can't get to grips with the fact that nosh like pizzas, burgers and pies can be meat-free and just as tasty.

'Isn't vegetarian food bland?'

Are they *kidding*?! Haven't these people ever heard of herbs or spices? Or maybe they've never heard of garlic! Just one clove can transform a meal in seconds, and if you crush it straight into the food instead of frying it first, it'll taste even stronger.

Mango sauce adds a sweet taste to any dish (but don't try it in puddings!), and if you really want to hot things up, a dash of chilli sauce will melt your tastebuds.

For some great ideas on using herbs and spices see page 67.

When you're flavouring food, don't just try to mimic meaty tastes and don't be afraid of trying brand-new flavours. Being veggie is a tongue-tickling, mouthwatering taste experience. Meat-eaters don't realize what they're missing.

'If everyone went vegetarian what would happen to all the animals?'

Well, first of all, it's highly unlikely that the whole world would become veggie at once. But as more and more people turn towards a vegetarian lifestyle and the demand for meat diminished, less animals will be bred for slaughter. Farm animals could live in peace in special sanctuaries or reserves without the threat of slaughter hanging over them. Land would be used to grow crops for human consumption, and there would be more land available for wildlife to flourish.

'Why don't you just have a little bit of meat'

The idea that a little bit of meat is any less disgusting than a huge piece seems rather silly. This question is particularly strange when followed by 'I won't tell anyone.'

'It's natural for humans to eat meat'

Oh no it isn't! Biologically, humans have a digestive system very similar to the higher primates – apes and monkeys – who survive perfectly well on a fruit and vegetable based diet. Meat eating is merely a habit, *not* a necessity.

'Do you eat chicken/fish?'

You'll get this a lot. Be patient with them and explain what vegetarian means. They'll probably then say 'I know a vegetarian who eats chicken.' Grit your teeth and start explaining all over again . . .

'How long are you going to be vegetarian?'

This dim question assumes you'll care about animals' lives for a bit, then forget about them completely and adopt your old habits again.

Some people do experiment to see whether a veggie lifestyle is the one for them, but most go veggie with the intention of keeping it up for life.

There are zillions of famous folk who are veggies, so if your mates insist on giving you hassle then just point out what good company you're in! Veggie celebs include Madonna, Michael Jackson, Bryan Adams, Paul and Linda McCartney, Chrissie Hynde, Morrissey, River Phoenix, Peter Gabriel, Tony Benn MP, Yehudi Menuhin, Marie Helvin, Jimmy Somerville, Dannii Minogue, James, London Beat, Rebel MC, . . . and over 3.6 million people in Britain including YOU!

Tips for easy conversions

1 Don't pester people to go veggie – you don't want them to think being vegetarian means being a bore;
2 Explain yourself, and your reasons – eventually logic will prevail;
3 Cook them tasty veggie meals every now and again – make them know what they're missing;
4 Try a bit of bribery and corruption – it never fails;
5 Ask them when are they going to eat their cat;

6   If all those fail but you're stubborn enough to keep trying, there is one thing which apparently works every time. The Vegetarian Society have made a video, *Food Without Fear*, which is so graphic and persuasive that almost everyone who watches it is instantly converted. You can borrow it free (with a small deposit. See p.152 for the Society's address). If you get permission, you may even be able to show the video at school.

Hassle from mates

These days being veggie is so normal and right-on that you're not likely to have to justify your actions but you may get the odd mate who insists on trying to pick holes in your logic and prove you're a hypocrite or a woolly idealist – tough task! This sort of person is usually feeling pretty guilty themselves so don't hesitate to attack back. It's hard to be 100% veggie in our world – after all, even shopping in a big supermarket is supporting an animal–killing institution – but you know you're doing all you can to prevent unnecessary suffering and save the planet. Your mate can't say that so why are they attacking you? Hit back by challenging them to watch The Vegetarian Society's videos 'Food without Fear' and 'SCREAM' with you.

Hassle at school

Just occasionally, young veggies have trouble with home economics teachers wanting them to cook with meat or science teachers insisting they dissect animals.
YOU DON'T HAVE TO DO THIS!
If your teachers are so unthinking as to force you, first of all try and explain calmly and clearly why you don't want to. Don't fight or get aggressive, just explain that it's against your principles. If they still won't listen, take it to the head, always keeping calm and logical. If necessary, involve your parents, and contact The Vegetarian Society who can offer a

lot of support including offering to come and give a talk to your class. You could also consider contacting the National Council for Civil Liberties (it's your *right* not to touch meat), your local paper or your local MP.

Greenscene

If there are times when you feel no one is on your side or if you just fancy a bit of information and a good read, the junior brand of The Vegetarian Society is really worth joining. It only costs £4 a year and you get their brilliant magazine *Greenscene* four times a year. This is packed with good articles, recipes, hints and information and has a great penfriends section full of like-thinking veggies for you to contact. We really recommend becoming a member!

13

EATING OUTSIDE THE HOME

At school

Fortunately, most schools these days are really good at dealing with special dietary requirements, and you should have no trouble getting the sort of food you can eat. Whether it's the sort you *like* to eat is another matter – but if all you're being offered is greasy cheese pasties, you can always switch to packed lunches, which have the added advantage that you know exactly what goes into them.

Don't be afraid to speak to your head or to the school cook and explain exactly what you can and cannot eat. Don't assume you're asking too much – most cooks will be glad to be kept fully informed. If you want to be sure that the cheese isn't made with rennet or food doesn't contain animal fat, you have to let the school know about this.

If you think your cook isn't very on the ball about vegetarian food and could do with some extra information, then send off for a free CHOICE! pack, which includes information sheets, stickers and a poster, plus a four week vegetarian recipe book that you can wave under your cook's nose. The CHOICE! campaign is run by The Vegetarian Society and aims to encourage schools to provide healthy meat-free meals. Contact The Vegetarian Society for further details – their address can be found on page 152.

If you're unlucky enough to come up against a cook of the 'I can't be dealing with these fads' school of cooking – and you *will* be unlucky if you do – then ask your parents to have a word with the head. It's your right to be vegetarian and you deserve support in this. If the school still won't budge, write to your local paper and make an issue of it. But don't worry – it's very, very unlikely to happen.

Packed lunch recipes

If your school doesn't have a proper vegetarian option at lunch-time, or if it does but it's just as horrible as the traditional school dinners, you may decide to take a packed lunch. Sandwiches are definitely the easiest thing to make, but things like cold pizza and veggie slices make a change every so often. You could make them at the weekend and keep them wrapped in the fridge until you use them up, or you could have them hot for tea and take the leftovers to school the next day.

Sandwich fillings

It's sometimes hard to think of exciting new combinations to put in sandwiches, particularly if you're used to ham and salami. So here are a few suggestions to pack your lunch with a punch. (The cream cheese and the hard cheese can be made from soya if you're vegan.)

Peanut butter and celery

Thinly spread both slices of bread with margarine (if you like) and peanut butter. Chop a stick of celery into very small pieces and sprinkle them over one slice of bread, then put the other on top (why are we telling you this? We're quite sure you know how to make a sandwich). The taste of celery goes really well with peanut butter and it makes the sandwich less stodgy.

Marmite and peanuts

Just make an ordinary Marmite sandwich and scatter the nuts in whole. Delicious! It's better to use unsalted peanuts for this as Marmite's very salty already.

Cream cheese and peppers

You can use either cream cheese or Quark for this. Spread it quite thickly, cover with thinly-sliced red or green peppers and grind some black pepper on top – delicious!

Cheese, tomato and mustard

Spread one slice of bread with mayonnaise or egg-free dressing. Slice the cheese and tomato and lay on top, then cover the other slice with mustard.

Mayonnaise or margarine makes bread more waterproof because it's oily, so make sure the side the tomato is on is well covered with mayonnaise – because there's no sandwich worse than a wet and watery tomato one (except perhaps a wet, watery and pink beetroot one).

Cottage cheese, paprika and spring onions

Cottage cheese is also good at making bread soggy so make sure you waterproof it well with margarine or mayo. Mix the cheese with a bit of paprika, or cayenne if you want it to be even hotter, and sprinkle it with finely chopped spring onion. Hot stuff!

Tahini, soy sauce and cucumber . . .

Mix a dessertspoonful of tahini and a teaspoonful of soy sauce in an egg-cup. Spread it on to both bits of bread and put some finely sliced cucumber in the middle.

Salads and slices

Pasta salad

Cook a couple of ounces (about 50 g) of pasta shells or twists. Drain and leave to cool. Dice a handful of vegetables, but be careful which ones you choose: things like lettuce, cress and cucumber go soggy and disgusting if they're left sitting in salad dressing for more than a few hours – especially at room temperature. Use hard vegetables like carrots, celery, cauliflower, pepper, broccoli and spring onions.

Dress the salad with mayonnaise, egg-free dressing or vinaigrette (oil and vinegar), then spoon the salad into a plastic pot with a tight-fitting lid.

Pizza

This is a very easy pizza recipe. You make the base with self-raising flour instead of yeast, so it's not quite the same as the pizza you buy, but it is just as tasty.

Ingredients

For the base	*For the topping*
25 g (1 oz) margarine	pepper
a pinch of salt	200 g (7 oz) tin tomatoes
225 g (8 oz) self-raising flour	1 small onion
275 ml (½ pint) milk or water	50 g (2 oz) cheese

Optional – green or red pepper (sliced), sweetcorn, mushrooms, olives, capers, garlic, herbs or anything else you like to add to your topping.

1. Rub the margarine, salt and flour together with the tips of your fingers.
2. Add the milk or water a little at a time and mix it in with your fingers. When it's soft and doughy (use more or less liquid if you have to) pat it with flour and press it into a flat circle until it is about 10mm (½ inch) thick.
3. Place on a greased baking dish and grind some salt and pepper on top.
4. Blend or finely chop the tomatoes and spread them over the base. Slice the onion and scatter it on top of the tomato. (If you are using any optional ingredients, put them on now.)
5. Grate the cheese and sprinkle it over the whole lot.
6. Bake in the oven at gas mark 5, 190°C for twenty to thirty minutes, until the cheese is bubbling and golden.

Obviously you can eat this dish hot, but it's also good cold at lunchtime. And if you cover it, it can stay in the fridge for a few days.

Cheesy lentil slice

225g (8 oz) red lentils
425 ml (¾ pint) water
100 g (4 oz) cheese or tofu
cheese
OR 1 tblsp gram flour and
1 tblsp water

1 small onion
25g (1 oz) margarine
1 teaspoon mixed herbs
1 free-range egg
1 oz breadcrumbs

1. Cook the lentils in the water until they turn to a thick paste. (This should take about twenty-five minutes.)
2. Grate or finely chop the cheese.
3. Chop the onion and fry it in the margarine until it becomes transparent.
4. Mix the lentils, onion and all the other ingredients together, adding salt and pepper if you like.
5. Grease a 23 cm (9 inch) cake tin and pour in the mixture.
6. Bake for thirty minutes at gas mark 5 (190°C).
7. Slice like a cake and serve hot or cold.

This also makes a great meal with homemade tomato sauce (see page 91) and salad.

Dessert

Fresh or dried fruit makes an ideal lunchtime 'afters' snack, but if you fancy something a bit different try this:

Frozen yoghurt

Put a carton of yoghurt in the freezer overnight. Depending on how well heated your school is, when you come to eat it it will either be soft and icy, or thawed but cold, as if it's just come out of the fridge.

Other people's homes

The prospect of a veggie turning up for a meal can really freak some people out while others will love rising to the challenge. Either way, you should warn your hosts in good time beforehand or you could end up making a mad dash to the nearest chippie!

Assure them that there's really no need for panic – and insist that they don't make a special effort just for you. Suggest pasta or – everyone's favourite standby – an omelette. Or, if they're interested, lend them a veggie cookbook. Meat eaters often rise to the challenge and concoct wonderful veggie food.

Eating out

Most decent restaurants nowadays have a vegetarian dish on the menu. It may only be microwaved lasagne, but at least it's there. If there really isn't anything on the menu you can eat, you can always ask them to make you something – they'll usually offer you an omelette (probably made from battery farmed eggs).

If this doesn't sound too appetizing you could make up something from the ingredients you can see on the menu – green vegetables, potatoes and avocado with cottage cheese, for example. Ask very nicely and they will almost always do it for you. Don't worry if the staff seem to think you're a bit eccentric – so long as you ask nicely, most restaurants will do something special for you. Being a bit of a nuisance has got to be better than eating omelettes every time you go out to dinner!

The Vegetarian Society produces a Travel Guide which lists restaurants with good veggie menus – or there's also a book called 'Where to Eat if You Don't Eat Meat' published by Grafton. If you can't afford to buy this book, you'd probably find it in most libraries. You'll be amazed, once you start looking, how many excellent vegetarian restaurants there are around.

Indian restaurants

A large proportion of the population of India is vegetarian and they really understand what it means, so you're on safe ground here and you'll find lots of tasty foods to eat. There are also more and more Indian vegetarian restaurants springing up. Any you see that have 'bel-puri' in the title are likely to be vegetarian. But even an ordinary meaty Indian restaurant will give you lots of choice. Try *Mattir paneer* (spelling may vary), a creamy blend of soft cheese and peas; *Aloo ghobi*, spicy potatoes; *vegetable korma*, a delicious creamy mild curry; or *Masala dosa*, a papery stuffed pancake.

Chinese restaurants

You need to take care in Chinese restaurants as there is a strong tradition of frying foods in animal fats, such as chicken fat. So even a fried rice may not be vegetarian. And many otherwise veggie dishes will be cooked in meat stock. Beware of spring rolls which will probably have shrimps in, and special fried rice, which will have scraps of meat in. However, there are many Chinese Buddhists who are vegetarian and some restaurants have separate veggie menus, and make the most amazing tofu dishes! Always ask about vegetable dishes.

'Safe' restaurants

This is a list of what you can (and can't) eat in the fast-food and big chain restaurants. (All of these below may have vegetarian specials from time to time; the dishes mentioned are those that are regularly on the menu.)

Berni Inn – Quorn tikka masala – if you eat Quorn (which contains non-free range eggs); Pasta, broccoli and mushroom Alfredo; Salads.

McDonald's – Almost nothing. Their rolls and shakes are safe, and so are their salads but the chips are fried in beef fat, the apple pies are made with animal fat, and there's whey and egg in all sorts of other things. But this may change as they're reviewing their policies. They're very helpful so you can always give them a call and ask. You can pick up a booklet telling you what's in the food at any of their restaurants. But it doesn't really help, there are so many unrecognizable ingredients – like disodium dihydrogen diphosphate – so even if you read them, you'll still be none the wiser. Many vegetarians won't eat at Macdonalds because they are one of the biggest killers of animals in the world – worth thinking about even if your meal's veggie.

Pizza Express – Vegetable pizzas (without cheese, if you're a strict vegetarian, as the cheese is made with rennet).

Pizza Hut – Any non-meat pizza with mozarella on it (the mozarella is made with microbially-grown vegetarian rennet); Garlic bread; Salads. (Beware of any cheese-topped pizza with more than one type of cheese on it – they're called 'Feast' pizzas – as any cheeses other than the mozarella will contain animal rennet.)

Pizzaland – Meat-free pizzas (minus the cheese, if you don't eat rennet); Garlic bread; Salads.

Spud-U-Like – Potatoes filled with any of the following: baked beans; sweet corn; cottage cheese; butter; ratatouille. (Neither the cheddar nor coleslaw fillings are veggie, so don't try them.)

Wimpy – The 'Wimpy Food File' (available from most outlets) gives details of what goes into their meals, but beware of their 'meat-free' dishes. Their beanburgers are more often than not fried in the same oil as their beefburgers and chicken slices, so they are best avoided (they also have rennet-made cheese on top). Although the fries are supposed to be cooked in vegetable oil, they cannot *guarantee* it – so, once again, steer clear. They'll happily do you a brown or white bun with just salad in it for the same price as a burger – but the buns are made with animal fats. In fact, even their pies and ice-cream sundaes are made with animal fats.

On the motorway

Welcome Break – Here the vegetarian dishes are specially prepared by the Crank's vegetarian food chain, so you can be sure they're completely veggie. *Savouries*: Leek and pine-nuts cannelloni; Gratinated mixed bean ratatouille; Glazed mushroom and walnut pot bake. *Desserts*: Carrot cake; Flapjacks; Crunchy nut and raisin cookies; Sticky date cake; Raspberry and almond tart.

14

THE VEGGIE HOLIDAY SURVIVAL GUIDE

Yippee! School's out for summer . . . You've packed up your bucket and spade, smothered your bod with suncream (which hasn't been tested on animals, of course!), slipped your Walkman into your beachbag and you're all set to spend two weeks lazing around.

But hang on a second! – things aren't quite as groovy as they seem. You don't speak the lingo! So how are you going to survive, if you can't explain to bemused waiters that you're a veggie?

Don't panic! Going on holiday needn't be a disaster on the food front. First, it's always worth brushing up on a few key phrases for the country you're about to visit. Borrow a couple of phrasebooks from the library before you go, just to make doubly sure you're not going to go hungry. Check out, too, Andrew Sanger's book *The Vegetarian Traveller* (published by Grafton), which is packed with all sorts of useful info guaranteed to keep those hunger pangs away while you're abroad.

Taking precautions

Let's be honest, your folks aren't really going to base the family's holiday plans around your eating habits. But there are some simple steps you can take to make sure you won't come home looking like a stick insect.

If you're off on a package holiday, suggest to your parents that they let the tour operator know you're a vegetarian. The hotel can then arrange special meals for you. You could be on to a winner here, as often the veggie option is miles better than the usual food.

Making life easier

Self-catering holidays are obviously going to be simpler to deal with. You can load up with supplies of goodies like veggieburgers, pasta and tinned food, and check out the local markets for other goodies.

Once at your holiday destination you could always phone any restaurants you're planning to visit a day or so ahead, to let them know that you'll be requiring something special. Chefs are always keen to have a challenge in the kitchen so, again, you could end up with the nicest meal.

A word of warning: omelettes are everyone's favourite standby when there's a veggie on the loose. Try not to eat eggs at every meal because, apart from the obvious health risks (eggs are high in cholesterol), you might end up a bit whiffy – and this will do nothing to improve international relations!

Eating on aeroplanes

If you're going on a long flight (or even a short one) you can ask to be served a vegetarian meal. All you have to do is ring the airline a few days beforehand, tell them exactly which flight you're going to be on and what you don't want to eat. Nothing is too fussy. If you eat cheese but not eggs, just tell them. Your food will also be brought to you first and will probably be a lot nicer than everyone else's. Don't forget to tell them the time of your return flight as well.

Round-the-world veggie guide

Here's a quick round-the-world guide to countries you might find yourself holidaying in this summer, with tips on how to avoid going hungry and some useful phrases which might make the difference between having a gourmet meal and going hungry.

France

The French are famous for eating so-called 'delicacies' such as snails, frogs' legs, horse-meat and rabbit stew. But it's not all doom and gloom. Fortunately, they also make some of the most delicious cheeses in the world, and lots of soft ones which won't contain rennet. Warning: Brie and Camembert, though pretty soft by anyone's standards, do contain rennet.

If you're eating out, look carefully at the delicious hors d'oeuvres menu, where you'll probably find mouth-watering melons, avocados, artichokes, enormous salads and selections of vegetables. Why not ask for a sauce for your vegetables? – but check first that it hasn't been made with beef stock. Look out for *sauce provençal*, an absolutely gorgeous sauce made with tomatoes, garlic, herbs, aubergines, courgettes and peppers.

Another word of warning: vegetarianism isn't half as common in France as it is in Britain – so be prepared to be treated as a complete loony!

Useful phrases
Do you have any vegetarian dishes? – *Est-ce que vous faites des plats végétariens?*
I am vegetarian – *Je suis végétarian*

We are vegetarian – *Nous sommes végétarien*
I don't want meat or fish – *Je ne veut pas de la viande ou du poisson*
No meat/fish/egg/cheese/meat stock/fish stock – *Pas de viande/poisson/oeuf/fromage/bouillon de viande/bouillon de poisson*

Germany and Austria

Vegetarianism has been popular in Germany and Austin since the last century. So you'll find quite a few vegetarian restaurants and health-food shops – useful if you're self-catering. In fact there's a veggie restaurant in Hamburg that's been open since 1865.

Sauerkraut (pickled cabbage) is a very popular dish and is usually vegetarian. Try *rosti*, too, a savoury cake made from fried grated potato and onion, which is a bit like bubble and squeak.

Food in Germany or Austria will often have been cooked in lard or meat stock, so do be careful. *Gemuseplatte*, boiled vegetables usually served in a creamy sauce, should be OK, but it's worth checking what sort of stock has been used.

Minced meat often turns up in dishes that sound as though they should be veggie, like cauliflower cheese, and most vegetable soups will have been made with meat stock. Don't order anything without checking first. If in doubt, ASK.

The best grub for veggies in these parts are the absolutely gorgeous cakes and biscuits. Spicy apple strudel, chocolate-coated biscuits and fruit pies with cream are well worth checking out, and they're usually made with butter.

Useful phrases

I am vegetarian – *Ich bin Vegetarier* (V is produced W and the G is hard, as in 'get')

We are vegetarian – *Wir sind Vegetarier* (W is pronounced V and sind is pronounced zint)

I don't want meat/fish – *Ich mochte keine Fleisch essen/ Fisch essen*

No egg/cheese/meat stock/fish stock – *Keine Ei/Käse/Fleischbruhe/Fischbruhe*

Is there a vegetarian restaurant near here? – *Gibt's ein vegetarisches Restaurant in dieser Gegend?*

Greece

Greece is a great place for veggies – although you may have to be careful at Easter, their main festival, when virtually everybody eats lamb (it's the equivalent of our Christmas turkey).

Greece is perfect for a meat-free holiday the rest of the year. *Hummus* (garlicky chick pea purée) *tzatziki* (yoghurt, garlic, herbs and cucumber), and *melitzanasalata* (an aubergine dip), make a delicious and filling meal with pitta bread and Greek salad. Watch out for *taramasalata*, a pinky-coloured dip. It's made from fish eggs and, unlike hens, the fish have to be killed in order to extract their eggs. Spinach and cream cheese in filo pastry, *spanakopita*, is served in most cafés; and our trusty friend, the omelette, is usually available if you're struggling.

Cakes are a must here, too. Most are made with nuts and honey instead of refined sugar, so they are healthier (even if they're fattening). Try *baclava* (also known as *paklava* and *baklava*), a flaky pastry drenched with honey, and *kataifa*, which is like shredded wheat drenched in honey and nuts.

Useful phrases

I don't want meat/fish – *Den thelo kreas / psari*

Without meat / fish / cheese – *Horis kreas / psari / tyri*

There isn't a Greek word for vegetarian. There is a word which means 'vegetable eater' but unfortunately it also means 'a bit loopy'!

Holland

Chips with mayonnaise are a popular Dutch delicacy but obviously it's not a good idea to scoff this for your entire holiday. Many fast-food places serve salad, and there are plenty of vegetarian cafés around. Standard restaurants usually have a veggie dish on the menu – look for the words *vegetarische schotel*. Keep an eye out for dishes like *bitterballsen* (potato croquettes with peanut sauce) and *huzarensalade* (boiled potatoes with mayonnaise, egg and pickle) – but do check that they haven't got meat in them. *Kaassouffle* means cheese soufflé and *witlof met kaassaus* is chicory in cheese sauce.

The Netherlands have a large population of Indonesians, and you can get some great Indonesian food like *bami* (noodles and vegetables) or *nasi goreng* (vegetables with rice).

Useful phrases

Do you have any vegetarian dishes? *Hebt u ook vegetarische schotels?*
I don't eat meat – *Ik ate geen vlees* (pronounced hain flais)
We don't eat meat – *Wij ate geen vlees*
No meat / fish/ animal fat – *Geen vlees/ vis/ dierlijk vet*

India

If you find yourself holidaying in India then you are in luck! India is one of the easiest places in the world to get vegetarian food. The cow is a sacred animal so beef is not served except in the growing number of burger bars there. Spicy vegetable stews, rices, *samosas* (vegetable pasties), *bhajis* (deep-fried vegetable balls) and *lassi* (yoghurt drinks) are sold everywhere.

Italy

Italians love food and plenty of it! There are a million and one different types of pasta and some of the most delicious sauces you'll taste anywhere. Check out *pasta alla boscaiola* (pasta with tomato, aubergine and mushroom), *alla cavalleggera* (with eggs, nuts and cream), *ai funghi* (with mushrooms), *alla Napoletana* (in tomato, olive oil and garlic), *al pesto* (with garlic, olive oil and basil), *al pomodoro* (with tomatoes) and *salsa verde* (with spinach).

Try *gnocci*, little dumplings which are a bit like pasta and made from potatoes and flour. If you're a pizza freak you'll be well catered for, too. You'll find an enormous selection of tempting toppings. But do be careful because Italian food very often has bits of ham, salami, anchovy or chicken in it.

Avoid parmesan cheese if you're a strict vegetarian, as it's always made with rennet.

Useful phrases
I am vegetarian – *Sono vegetariano*
We are vegetarian – *Siamo vegetariani*
No meat/fish/cheese/egg – *Niente carne/pesce* (pronounced carnay/peshay) / *formaggio/uovo*
No ham/anchovies – *Niente proscuitto / acciughe*

Portugal

It's rare to see a meal on a Portuguese menu that doesn't have fish or meat in it somewhere. But don't despair. Portuguese salads are absolutely fab and omelettes are available in most restaurants.

You can also find the most gorgeous stews in Portugal. *Grao* is a chickpea stew. There's *grao espinafres* or *grao con tomates* which are stews with chickpeas and spinach or tomatoes.

Check that the soups aren't made with meat or fish stock. Try *sopa de agrioes*, a watercress soup with cream and egg, and *sopa de tomate a alentejana*, which is garlicky tomato soup with a poached egg.

Portugal is famous for its pastries, especially those filled with thick, creamy custard.

Useful phrases

It's almost impossible to describe how these words are pro-
nounced – so just give it your best shot!
I am vegetarian – *Eu sou vegetariano*
We are vegetarian – *Nos somos vegetariano*
No meat/fish/cheese/eggs – *Nao carne/peixe/queijo/ovo*
Is there meat in this? – *Isto tem carne?*

Russia / Eastern Europe

Bad luck if you're off to Eastern Europe for your hols – the whole
region is not known for its vegetarian cuisine. Fresh vegetables
are rare, and those served are usually the ones that last the
longest without going mouldy, like cabbage and root vegetables.
But here goes, anyway . . .

The Russians' favourite soup is, of course, *borscht*, which
is beetroot soup and is actually much nicer than it sounds. (If
you believe *that* and want to try it, it's sometimes made with
meat stock so check first.) *Blinis* are small, thick pancakes
with cream cheese, and they're definitely delicious. Aubergine, mushroom and courgette 'caviar' (puréed vegetables with
onion, tomato, lemon and oil) are worth looking out for –
but steer clear of real caviar: not only is it expensive, it's
sturgeons' eggs.

If you've still found nothing to tickle your tastebuds, try
asking for vegetables with sour cream or cottage cheese and
rye bread. You might get some peppers stuffed with vegetables
if you're lucky, and Russian chocolate is quite good, too.

Sweet fruit soups, made with sour cream and cherries, apricots or wild berries are a good source of protein and are probably the only fresh fruit you'll find. And cheesecakes and sugary buns are useful to fill yourself up with if you don't get a proper meal.

Useful phrases
I am vegetarian – *Ya vegetarianets*
We are vegetarian – *Moy vegetariantsai*
Without meat/fish/egg/cheese/caviar – *Byez myasa/ribi/yaitsa/ sir/ikri*
Is there meat in this? – *Yest myaso v etom?*

Spain

There will always be something for you to eat in Spain but it won't necessarily be inspiring. Luckily, it's possible to live for quite a while on a diet of bread, cheese, omelettes and salad – because if you go to Spain you might have to! Try to eat fresh fruit whenever you can, and gobble up the odd packet of nuts before a meal for a balanced diet.

Tapas are delicious little snacks that will fill you up in no time, and some are vegetarian. You're safe with *aceitunas* (olives), *alcachofas* (artichokes), *almendras tostadas* (toasted almonds), *champiñónes* (mushrooms), *ensalada valenciana* (a salad of rice, tomatoes and peppers), *gazpachŏ* (cold salad soup), *patatas bravas* (spicy potatoes), *quesos* (bread and cheese) and *tortilla* (hot or cold potato omelette).

In the more touristy areas you'll probably be able to get spaghetti and pizza; and if you're on a self-catering holiday and look hard, you might find a couple of health-food shops.

Useful phrases

Do you have any vegetarian dishes? – *Tiene algún plato vegetariano?*
I am vegetarian – *Soy vegetariano*
We are vegetarian – *Somos vegetarianos*
I (we) cannot eat meat or fish – *No puedo (podemos) comer carne ni pescado*
No meat/fish/cheese/eggs – *No carne/pescado/queso/heuvos*

Turkey

Turkish food is not dissimilar to Greek food. *Hummus* (garlicky chick-pen purée), *cacik* (yoghurt, cucumber and garlic, like Greek tzatziki and pronounced shashlik) and *beyaz peynir* (a cheese which is a lot like feta) are all very common. (Warning: Feta is not always veggie, so if in doubt, leave it out.)

Most of the main meals will have been made with meat (particularly goat or mutton) but loads of the starters (or *meze*, pronounced metsay) will be veggie.

Dolmas are vegetables or vine leaves stuffed with rice and herbs, they often contain minced meat, so do check. *Borek* are little pastries stuffed with either cheese or meat – just ask for the ones you want. *Imam bayildi* (aubergines stuffed with vegetables) and *pirincli ispanak* (rice baked with spinach in a tomato sauce) are delicious, too.

Turkish salads are good. Look for *coban salatasi*, which is cucumber, tomatoes, peppers and onion in olive oil and lemon dressing; and *karisik salata*, a mixed vegetable salad. A famous Turkish soup that's worth trying is *tarhana corbasi*, made from yogurt, thickened with flour, and mixed with tomatoes and pepper. And if you're really stuck there's *marul*, which is simply a whole lettuce served in a glass.

Useful phrases
Do you have any vegetarian dishes? – *Etsiz yemeğiniz var mih?*
(Etseez yeh-meh-eeneez var meh)
I am vegetarian – *Et yemez im*
We are vegetarian – *Et yemez iz*
Without meat/no meat – *Etsiz*
Without fish/no fish – *Baliksiz*

15

TEMPTATION

When you first become veggie you may occasionally be tempted to eat fish or meat. Tucking into a burger is bound to make you guilty and you probably won't enjoy it nearly as much as you used to – especially when you suddenly remember what it's made from!

Meat is packed with yukky toxins which your body grows used to over the years. After a few months of vegetarianism the poisins will have been flushed out of your system, and you may find that your stomach simply can't handle meat any more.

Quite often you may find that the temptation is not really caused by a desperate urge to eat meat, but because it seems easier to eat rather than make a fuss. Make sure you can spot situations where this is likely to happen and be prepared!

Rather than giving in to temptation completely, why not try ways around it – like eating a veggieburger. There are lots of varieties, including cheese, chilli-flavoured and curried veggieburgers.

Here are some typical pitfalls for new veggies to keep an eye out for:

With your mates

If all your buddies are trooping off to the local burger bar, you may find yourself stuck on your own if you don't go along too. And if you're starving hungry and surrounded by people stuffing their faces with greasy burgers, it might be very easy to slip

up and eat something you'll regret. Just remember, hardly any of the food available at fast-food restaurants is vegetarian (see p. 110). Even the chips will probably have been fried in beef fat or oil that's been used to cook meat.

Try to persuade your mates to go somewhere that serves veggie grub. If they won't, then perhaps it's about time you changed your mates!

The other alternative is to make you and your friends some hamburger substitutes at home. They're much tastier – not to mention cheaper. Load them up with dill pickles, mustard and ketchup and you won't miss a thing!

On your own

What happens when you're stuck in the house on your own and feeling peckish? There's salami in the fridge and chocolate biccies (made with animal fat) in the tin just crying out to be eaten.

You've coped with Sunday lunches and after-school visits to the burger bar and swanked to everyone about how good you're being, but now you only have yourself to answer to. Help!!

Well, first, it isn't the end of the world if you do crack, but you are going to feel very, very guilty afterwards. If you do feel you're going to give in, just think very carefully for a second about fluffy little lambs and big-eyed calves, about hens unable to move in their cramped conditions and about the horror of the slaughterhouse where the animals will end their miserable lives. Remember also that meat eaters are prone to all sorts of frightening diseases and that meat eating is destroying our planet.

That should put a stop to it!

16

LOVELIFE

It may sound a little melodramatic, but one of these days you may be faced with a dilemma – should you fall in love with a meat-eater?

Being veggie doesn't necessarily mean the kiss of death on romantic relationships – unless of course you really want it to! Some veggies will put up with a carnivorous partner – some even don't mind cooking flesh for their other halves while others will just show them the door. Of course, if you choose this latter option you could lessen your chances of love – remember that, at present in the UK, about one person in fourteen is veggie, so you'll be limiting your choice.

If you decide that life is unbearable without your meat-eating loved one, then you could always try to convert him/her. This, of course, has to be done very sneakily – so they don't actually realize what you're up to. Bribes and incentives are the key words here. For instance, cook a romantic veggie meal one evening for the love of your life – it can do wonders.

You don't have to limit yourself to converting your beloved – have a go with mum and dad and other members of the family, too. Try offering to wash the car one weekend in return for the family sampling a Sunday nut roast.

Kissing with confidence

Even if you do decide that, in theory, you can cope with a girlfriend or boyfriend who eats animals, can you cope in practice? There's nothing worse than getting a whiff of meaty breath when you've settled down for a good smooch. After all, you wouldn't snog your cat after he's scoffed a bowl of Whiskas so why should you be expected to get passionate with someone with pongy meat-breath? And having a quick snog with someone whose breath stinks of tuna has got to be one of the worst ways ever of passing the time!

If you really can't bear to get fruity with someone with animal breath then there are two possible options. Either make them eat mints or brush their teeth before they come within a mile of you (which rather kills off any romantic spontaneity) OR make sure you eat equally smelly food – onions, garlic or curry are excellent bets. There are three possible consequences:

1 – you'll both smell absolutely foul and thus cancel each other's smelly breath out;

2 – you'll have to make a pact – they stop eating meat when they see you and you'll stop eating pongy food;

3 – an extremely drastic option, admittedly – the snogging stops and you share a new hobby, like chess or train-spotting.

17

How not to
Wear an animal

Leather

Now you've made up your mind to become veggie you may well be wondering whether or not you should wear leather.

Many veggies justify wearing leather by saying that animals are killed for their meat and not their skin, and therefore leather is just a by-product of the slaughterhouse. But there are many veggies who refuse to wear leather *just because* it's a by-product of the slaughterhouse.

The slaughterhouse trade is a very rich and profitable one. Every last part of an animal killed in a slaughterhouse can be sold on and used in some way. The flesh will be sold for meat; the skin will be made into leather, suede and sheepskin; and the horns, hooves and bones will be used to make gelatine. Even eyes are sold to schools for science experiments.

Luxury suede comes from the skin of unborn calves taken from slaughtered pregnant cows. Cow hide comes from dairy cattle that are past their 'usefulness' and are unable to meet their milk quotas. In fact, the leather trade is so lucrative that fur traders are giving up their businesses and moving into it.

Think about it: fur and leather are essentially the same product – animal skin.

Shoes

So should you wear leather or shouldn't you? Shoes pose a particularly awkward dilemma. To be quite honest, it's hard to give advice. The Vegetarian Society's policy on leather is Don't Wear It – and fortunately, these days there are some pretty good alternatives around.

Plastic and synthetic shoes are cruelty-free, but since they're made from oil by-products and are non-biodegradable, they aren't too helpful on the ecology front. Not only that, synthetic shoes prevent air getting to your feet – which is not only bad news for your poor feet but pretty hard on everybody else, too, since they don't exactly leave your feet smelling of roses! Research is being carried out to tackle this 'pongy' problem, so it shouldn't be too long before we see non-leather shoes which will allow your feet to breathe and end the sweaty sock syndrome. Meanwhile, we suggest you cruise the High

Street shops looking for styles that you feel you can live with happily that say 100% man made.

Canvas shoes are a good option in summer but you have to be careful about which type you buy, because the soles are often stuck on with cow gum (which is just as non-veggie as leather).

However many veggies do resort to wearing leather shoes. You can almost justify owning a couple of pairs by saying it's better to have one or two hard-wearing pairs of leather shoes than to stomp your way through hundreds of non-biodegradable ones. But, let's face it, this really is admitting defeat.

If you're determined not to wear leather then all credit to you. Try contacting the Vegan Society, who supply info on shops that offer good vegetarian alternatives to leather (see p.152 for their address). There's also Vegetarian Shoes, who make handmade, breathable, smart and casual styles. Contact them at Dept 8, 36 Gardner St, Brighton BN1 1UN. You can get veggie hiking boots from: Designer Wares, 8 Ashwell Rd, Bradford BD9 4AU.

Fur

Fur is not glamorous; fur is not fashionable; fur is not a status symbol. Recent surveys have consistently revealed that seven out of every ten people in the UK are opposed to the killing of animals for fur. Yet some of the world's most beautiful animals are in danger of becoming extinct because people insist on wearing it.

The main areas for fur hunting are North America, Scandinavia and Russia (Russia is responsible for supplying most of the world's fox and sable fur). With four hundred million animals killed annually worldwide, the hunting of wildlife for fur has led to a drastic reduction in the numbers of some species, and many are in danger of becoming extinct.

These horrifying statistics have been supplied by the anti-fur campaigners Advocates for Animals (see p.149 for their address).

Each year:
★ up to thirty million animals are trapped in the United States, Canada and Russia alone;
★ sixty thousand ermine are trapped;
★ one hundred thousand British and Irish red foxes are snared;
★ between three and four million raccoons are trapped in the United States and Canada.

Furs are beautiful, but only on their rightful owners.

How an animal is trapped

Contrary to what you might have thought, wild animals are not hunted and shot down, as bullet holes and pellets would damage their fur. The most commmon method of capturing wild animals is by the gin, or leghold trap. This particular trap was banned in the UK more than thirty years ago because it is such a barbaric contraption. Ironically, though, there's nothing to prevent companies here from importing skins from countries where the trap is still used, and British firms still manufacture these primitive traps for export.

When an animal stands on a gintrap the steel jaws snap tight shut around its leg. But the agony doesn't end there – the painwracked victim can be lying helpless for days before the trapper turns up to collect his prey. During that time the animal may try to gnaw off the trapped limb in a futile bid to escape from the device. The trapper will then kill the prey by either clubbing, strangulation, or suffocating the animal by standing on its vital organs.

These traps often catch unwanted animals, such as cats, dogs, owls and other birds. As Advocates for Animals points out, for every wild animal killed for the fur trade at least two others are killed and discarded as 'trash' animals.

There is some good news however. The charity Beauty without Cruelty have recently succeeded in getting the EC to agree to a ban on all wild-caught furs being imported into the EC from 1994/5. Campaigning does have an efect!

Fur farming

The fur trade is also amply supplied by the forty million animals – mainly mink and Arctic foxes – reared annually worldwide in small battery cages on fur farms. Here the animals' welfare is secondary to profit. The cages have no fresh air or sunlight,

There are thirty-one mink factory farms in the UK.

and the animals are unable to move around freely. Their lives are terminated by fatal injection, carbon monoxide poisoning or electrocution.

Other non-food animal products

Apart from wearing fur coats (which, of course, *you* don't!) and leather shoes, there are lots of other ways in which we use animal products in our daily lives – sometimes without even realizing it.

Gelatine

Many types of pills and tablets will be coated in a gelatine-based sac – to help them slip down more easily. Gelatine is made from the boiled-up bones of animals. If your doctor prescribes you gelatine-based capsules ask for an alternative.

It is possible that your doctor might be unable to supply you with an alternative to gelatine-based capsules. If so, you MUST take the medicines your doctor has prescribed.

Duck feathers

Pillows and continental quilts may be cosy and comforting, but not when they've been filled with down or feathers, a by-product of the slaughterhouse. There are lots of synthetic alternatives – go for them.

In the bathroom

Soaps are often made with animal fat, so check the label very carefully when you buy. The same goes for shampoos, which often contain gelatine.

Natural sponges are just as much a living animal as a cat or dog, so try to make do with a synthetic one or use a flannel. And if you shave with the old-fashioned type of razor, check that your shaver brush is not made with badger or dog hair.

Cosmetics

Ingredients are rarely listed on toiletries and cosmetics. Every day people slap slaughterhouse by-products on their faces and bodies without being aware of it. Many lipsticks and eyeliners, for example, contain animal fats, and most moisturizers are made from a blend of animal fat, water and chalk. If they don't contain animal fats then they're likely to have used petrochemical by-products instead as a base. These may be veggie but they're not very good for you – it's been estimated that thirty to fifty per cent of the population have some allergic reaction to them. So for the sake of your skin and the environment (the petrochemical industry is a major source of world pollution) it's a good idea to steer clear of petroleum jellies and mineral oils – go for vegetable oil products instead.

If you're in any doubt as to what your favourite cosmetics are made of, you could try contacting the manufacturer. Otherwise, switch to using cosmetics from well-established animal-free product manufacturers such as The Body Shop, Cosmetics To Go, or Beauty Without Cruelty (now available in most health-food shops).

The Body Shop has info available in all their shops telling you what their products are made of. (They do use petrochemicals in some of their products, so it's worth checking the ingredients if you want to avoid those.)

Sport and leisure

If you're into DIY or a budding artist, make sure your paintbrushes aren't made from sable hair. If you're sporty, choose your tennis and badminton rackets carefully, since the handles are often covered with suede for grip. Tennis rackets are frequently strung with catgut, too, which comes from the intestines of sheep. And remember that other types of equipment, such as footballs and rugby balls, are often made of leather.

These are just some of the things to watch out for. For more info on nasty products to watch out for, The Vegetarian Society has produced a list of 'Vegetarian Stumbling Blocks'. (Their address is on p.152 – and you'll need to send an SAE.) Or check out the even more comprehensive list printed in their book *'The Vegetarian Handbook'*.

18

ANIMAL EXPERIMENTS

How would you feel if someone wanted to poison your dog, pour shampoo into your rabbit's eyes or burn your gran's cat? Wouldn't you be horrified just at the thought of someone deliberately injuring your pet? Yet animals we keep as pets – rabbits, mice, rats, cats and dogs – are used daily in unnecessary tests on products designed to make us and our homes look and smell good.

Three million animals are experimented on annually in the UK, on products ranging from tobacco and alcohol to food additives and nerve gas. Many of these experiments are performed while the animals are fully conscious.

Over 12,000 animals were used to test cosmetics and toiletries in British laboratories in 1989 alone, and most large cosmetic companies still test their products on animals.

Here are just some of them:

The Draize Eye-test

Have you ever experienced that awful burning sensation when you've got shampoo in your eyes? Horrible, isn't it? How about if someone trapped your head in a collar and *then* dripped shampoo into your eyes? Well, this is exactly what happens to rabbits in the Draize Eye-test.

The Draize Eye-test is a test designed to monitor irritancy. The rabbits are held in a restraining collar, unable to move, while substances are dripped into their eyes. The effects, which include swelling, redness and blindness, are carefully monitored for anything up to seven days. Rabbits don't cry and, unlike humans, don't have proper tearducts so they are unable to wash these irritants from their eyes.

Skin irritancy tests

Skin irritancy tests are normally carried out on guinea pigs, rabbits or rats. In order to test how a certain substance might irritate human skin, the animal's back is first shaved of its fur, then the substance being tested is rubbed into its bare skin. The effects, which can include swollen and sore skin, are monitored for up to two weeks.

The LD 50 test

In the 'Lethal Dose 50%' (LD 50) test, a group of animals will be either force-fed or injected with a particular substance in order to find out what is the minimum dosage that will kill half their number. Pleasant, huh?

In 1989 BUAV (the British Union for the Abolition of Vivisection) commissioned a nationwide poll to find out how the public felt about the use of animals to test cosmetics and toiletries. Not surprisingly, there was massive opposition to animal testing.

★ 85 per cent of those polled gave the thumbs down to animal testing of toiletries and cosmetics;

★ 88 per cent felt that cosmetics and toiletries should clearly state whether or not they have been tested on animals;

★ 72 per cent were either very confident or fairly confident that a cosmetic or toiletry product which had not been tested on animals would be safe to use;

★ 66 per cent were prepared to pay more for a product which guaranteed that it had not been tested on animals;

★ 92 per cent thought that household products, such as bleach, washing powder and furniture polish, should not be tested on animals.

Cruelty-free high-street shopping

At long last companies finally seem to be getting the message that animal testing is not only cruel but unnecessary. Many of the big retail companies no longer test any of their own-brand cosmetics, toiletries or household products on animals. (They do sometimes sneak in the odd bit of animal fat and gelatine, though, so read the labels carefully.) Some even donate large sums towards finding alternatives to animal testing.

The following are some of the big name chainstores who have a policy not to test their own-brand products on animals:
Asda (their 'ABC' range of cosmetics contains no meat by-products either)
Boots
Marks and Spencer
Safeway
Sainsbury
Tesco

How can you be sure?

The fact is, even if a product has been labelled 'Not tested on animals', you cannot always be sure that the product's constituents, or raw materials, were never animal-tested at some time in the past.

Look out for the British Union for the Abolition of Vivisection (BUAV) 'Not-tested-on-animals' white rabbit logo. This shows that neither the finished product nor raw materials have been tested on animals within the past five years.

Some companies, such as Tesco, clearly label their own-brand products showing on each one whether it has *never* been tested on animals or whether it has not been animal-tested within the past five years.

If you're still not sure . . .

The BUAV has produced an *Approved Product Guide*, listing over two hundred cruelty-free cosmetic, toiletry and household product manufacturers. The guide is available free (see p.150 for their address).

If you're still not sure where it's safe to shop, buy from established cruelty-free manufacturers. Most health-food shops now sell not only ethically sound cosmetics and toiletries but also household products, such as bleaches, washing powders and cleaning fluids.

The Alternatives

Of course, it's essential that products are tested for their safety before they hit the shops. But there is no need for companies to continue with pointless experiments on animals when there are cruelty-free alternatives available.

Fortunately, manufacturers are beginning to realize this. Some are now relying on human volunteers to monitor safety; others use cells from human skin which are grown in a test-tube in order to find out how human skin will react to a product.

Many manufacturers simply rely on natural ingredients from plants and herbs, such as lavender, jojoba and honey, that have been used safely for thousands of years.

Cruelty-free shopping checklist

★ When buying toiletries and cosmetics make sure you only buy those which clearly state that the product has not been tested on animals and does not contain any animal derivatives;

★ Labels can be very misleading. The finished product may not have been tested on animals but the component ingredients may have been;

★ It's wrong to assume that products boasting cruelty-free labels are vegetarian. They may contain slaughterhouse by-products;

★ Double-check cleaning products. There are many environmentally-friendly household cleaners but not all are vegetarian or cruelty-free.

Next time you're pouting in front of the mirror practising your Madonna pose in your latest lipstick or trying to be Julian Clary, just think carefully about the true cost of beauty.

How you can help to stop animal testing for good

★ Refuse to buy any product that may have been tested on animals;

★ Write to pressure groups (listed at the back of the book);

★ If in doubt, buy products which clearly show the BUAV white rabbit logo;

★ Borrow from the library, or buy, a copy of *The Cruelty-Free Shopper* by Liz Howlett, (published by Bloomsbury).

Do keep in mind, too, that a product may not have been tested on animals but may still have animal products in it, like gelatine or fat. Many people who object to testing products on animals don't mind if animals are killed to provide ingredients for the finished article.

19
MEDICAL RESEARCH

We're all familiar with them – the hardy collectors who stand outside the supermarkets and train stations rattling their collection boxes in our faces, in the hope that we'll contribute some of our hard-earned dosh to the medical research charities they're representing.

Most of us will drop a bit of change into their tins and toddle off, sporting the charity sticker and feeling proud that we're doing our bit towards an end to human suffering and the progress of medical science. All well and good, so far.

But what you probably don't know is that many of the large medical charities are probably using a big part of your donation to fund animal experiments.

Over one million animals are used every year in the UK in medical experiments.

How reliable are animal medical experiments?

Every new drug is tested on animals, but it's impossible, even for the experts, to judge how humans will react to the same drug. A drug may be effectively tested on animals, but it won't necessarily give the same results in humans.

Take the drugs Eraldin, Opren, Osmosin and Flosint, for examples. Each of these were successfully tested on animals but caused horrendous side-effects – even death in some cases – on the human patients that were prescribed them. Conversely, animals can react badly to drugs that might be perfectly harmless and useful to humans.

To demonstrate how unreliable animal testing is, just look at these examples:

★ Penicillin kills hamsters and guinea pigs but frequently saves humans lives;
★ Morphine sedates humans but causes frenzied behaviour in cats;
★ Chloroform, an anaesthetic for humans, kills dogs;
★ Aspirin causes deformities in dogs, cats and rats – but not in humans.

So isn't it crazy to cage and perform experiments on defenceless animals in order to obtain frequently misleading results?

If you want to know more about this issue and about alternatives to animal testing, contact the British Union for the Abolition of Vivisection or Advocates for Animals (their addresses are on p. 149 & 150).

Around ninety-five per cent of new drugs that successfully pass the animal experiment stage are rejected after the second stage, when they have been tested on humans.

20

ACTION

If you feel strongly about animal rights or the environment, then you may like to join one of the many pressure groups around or even, perhaps, start up one of your own at school. The Vegetarian Society has produced a cracking booklet, *Ideas For Campaigning,* packed with sound ideas for campaigning both in and out of school. (see p.152 for their address.)

Action at school

If you decide to start an action group, then try to get the support of a sympathetic teacher who will support what you are up to. It just makes things a lot easier in the long run if a responsible adult knows what you're doing.

Your first meeting

Let everyone know the place and time of the first meeting of your group and design special posters to stick up around the school. Perhaps you could organize a competition to decide on the group's name and charge those entering 20p a go – the winning name gets the dosh!

It's useful to draw up an agenda of items for discussion before your first meeting. Then you'll need to sort out who you are going to choose to be special officers of the group. You should have a chair- or spokesperson; a secretary to record details of meetings; and a treasurer to collect subs (if you're going to charge for membership) and any money raised.

Many veggie and animal rights organizations will let you have free leaflets to dish out to your group and posters for the school noticeboards. Check that you can put these up first, otherwise you may find yourself involved in all sorts of running battles with your teachers, who could easily just ban your group from getting together before it's even got off the ground properly.

Getting the message across

Once you're started there's lots you can do. Write to local factory farmers; companies who stock animal-tested products; department stores who sell fur – the list is endless. Tell them just how strongly you feel about what they're doing. But try not to make your letter a torrent of abuse – your good intentions could well backfire. Check spellings and punctuation and try to make your letter as neat as possible.

If you're lucky enough to have a video machine at school, you could arrange a special viewing of the many animal rights films available from campaigning pressure groups. Some charge a hire cost; others, like The Vegetarian Society, only charge for postage plus a returnable deposit. You could find yourself with many converts by showing one of the many animal abuse films currently available.

If you have a school newspaper or newsletter, persuade the Editor to let you have a veggie column each issue. This is a great way of keeping the rest of the school informed and recruiting more members.

If your school doesn't have a newsletter, why not start your own? If you have access to a typewriter or word processor and a photocopier, it shouldn't be too much hassle. Invite contributions from members of the group on specific veggie issues, such as animal testing and facts about animal abuse. Include some simple veggie recipes and even, perhaps, a survey – you could do a poll on how many veggies there are in the school, for example.

How about dropping a press release to the local papers, TV and radio stations, telling them about your group and its aims? Perhaps they would like to sit in on one of your meetings? You never know, you may find yourself grinning at thousands of readers from the pages of the local rag or speaking to the town over the airwaves! It's worth a try, at least.

Fundraising

Is there an organization you particularly sympathize with? You could try to raise much-needed funds to help them continue with their campaigning work.
Here are some fund-raising ideas:

★ Organize a really whacky sponsored event;
★ Stage a talent contest, charging people to enter. Or how about organizing your own version of *Blind Date*?! (Get the teachers involved, too, for guaranteed laughs);
★ An end of term bop is *bound* to raise cash. Sell tickets and run games and raffles throughout the evening.

Addresses

If you would like further information on animal protection or the environment, write to one of the organizations below. Many of them have youth sections, and most will send you free information, leaflets and posters. Do enclose postage costs when requesting material.

Advocates for Animals
10 Queensferry St
Edinburgh EH2 4PG
(*Information on animal rights, vivisection, the fur trade.*)

Animal Aid
7 Castle St
Tonbridge
Kent TN9 1BH
(*Information on vegetarianism, animal rights, vivisection.*)

Animals' Defenders
Ravenside
Goldhawk Road
London W12 9PE
(*The youth arm of the National Anti-Vivisection Society. Information on animal rights, factory farming, circuses, zoos, the fur trade, vivisection.*)

Athene Trust
3A Charles Street
Petersfield
Hampshire GU32 3EH
(*Campaigns for humane animal slaughter – if animal slaughter could ever be called humane!*)

Beauty Without Cruelty Charity
57 King Henry's Walk
LONDON N1 4NH
(*Campaigns against all animal exploitation, particularly in connection with fashion and beauty.*)

Beauty without Cruelty Ltd
37 Avebury Avenue
Tonbridge
Kent TN9 ITL
(*Supplies cosmetics which have not been tested on animals.*)

BUAV (British Union for the Abolition of Vivisection)
16a Crane Grove
Islington
London N7 8LB
(*Anti-vivisection campaigners. Will supply list of 200 household products and cosmetics that haven't been tested on animals.*)

CALF (Campaign Against Leather and Fur)
PO Box 17
198 Blackstock Road
London N5 1EN
(*Will supply lots of useful information on fur and leather trades.*)

Campaign for the Abolition of Angling
PO Box 130
Sevenoaks,
Kent TN14 5NR
(*Anti-angling campaigners.*)

Compassion in World Farming
20 Lavant Street,
Petersfield
Hants GU32 3EW
(*Gives information about factory farming.*)

Dr Hadwen Trust for Humane Research
6c Brand St
Hitchin
Herts SG5 1HX
(*Funds research without animal experiments and can provide information about experiments and their alternatives.*)

Elefriends
Cherry Tree Cottage
Coldharbour
Near Dorking
Surrey RH5 6HA ·
(*Elephant protection group.*)

FRAME (Fund for the Replacement of Animals in Medical Experimentation)
Eastgate House
34 Stoney Street
Nottingham NG1 1NB
(*Information on medical experimentation alternatives.*)

Friends of the Earth
26/28 Underwood St
London N1 7JQ
(*Information on environmental campaigns.*)

Greenpeace
30–31 Islington Green
London N1 8XE
(*Information on environmental campaigns.*)

Fox Cubs
PO Box 1
Carlton
Notts. NG4 2JY
(*Junior wing of the Hunt Saboteurs Association. Campaigns actively against hunting.*)

League Against Cruel Sports (LACS)
83–87 Union Street
London SE1 1SG
(*Information on blood sports.*)

LYNX
PO Box 300
Nottingham NG1 5HN
(*Campaigns against the fur trade.*)

PDSA (People's Dispensary for Sick Animals)
South Street
Dorking
Surrey RH4 2LB
(*Treats sick animals – pets belonging to the unemployed get free treatment!*)

RSPCA (Royal Society for the Prevention of Cruelty to Animals)
Causeway
Horsham
West Sussex
(*Campaigns for animal welfare. Can send you lists of things that haven't been tested on animals and leaflets about animal abuse.*)

The Vegan Society
7 Battle Road
St Leonard's-on-Sea
East Sussex TN37 7AA
(*Information on veganism. Gives advice and information about going vegan and supplies lots of useful information on non-leather shoes, vegan foods, etc.*)

The Vegetarian Society
Parkdale
Dunham Rd,
Altrincham,
Cheshire, WA14 4QG
(*Supplies information on vegetarianism and all aspects of animal rights. The junior branch of the Society only costs £4 a year to join*

and you'll get loads of info & a free magazine 'Greenscene' four times a year. Runs special campaigns – e.g Choice!, the campaign for vegetarian school food. Supplies posters, leaflets and videos eg SCREAM, a brilliant video against factory farming)

Zoo Check
Cherry Tree Cottage,
Coldharbour
Dorking,
Surrey RH5 6HA
(Campaigns against the abuse of captive animals and wildlife.)

Index